THE
COUNTRY
HOUSE
AT WAR

THE
COUNTRY
HOUSE
AT WAR

Fighting the Great War at home and in the trenches

Simon Greaves

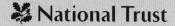

Dedicated to Barbara Mollison (1944–2014),
National Trust volunteer at Ightham Mote.

First published in the United Kingdom in 2014 by National Trust Books
1 Gower Street
London
WC1E 6HD

An imprint of Pavilion Books Company Ltd

ISBN: 9781907892776

A CIP catalogue record for this book is available from the British Library.

10 9 8 7 6 5 4 3 2 1

Reproduction by Mission Productions Ltd, Hong Kong
Printed and bound by 1010 Printing Ltd, China

This book can be ordered direct from the publisher at the website:
www.pavilionbooks.com, or try your local bookshop. Also available at
National Trust shops and www.shop.nationaltrust.org.uk

Page 2: Three Sergeants recover at Stamford Military Hospital at Dunham
Massey, Cheshire.

Contents

INTRODUCTION

The First World War touched every family in Britain and its impact on country houses reflected the damage across a nation. Rich and poor suffered equally. Living at Chirk Castle from 1911 was Thomas Scott-Ellis, Lord Howard de Walden, a man of enormous wealth, while on his estate Edward Hughes was being brought up by a widowed mother with five children in a decrepit three-room cottage. Edward left school at thirteen and went to work on one of Lord Tommy's farms for seven shillings per week. In different ways, the war cost both men dear. This book will explore its effect on the people who lived and worked on properties that later became part of the National Trust.

'Country house' is a loose term. It includes medieval castles such as Chirk, but ranges equally from the eighteenth century Palladian grandeur of Clandon Park to the more intimate Greys Court, a delightful building assembled over centuries. The National Trust is, of course, more than just country houses. In its care are TE Lawrence's tiny cottage at Clouds Hill, Max Gate and Shaw's Corner, the comfortable but unostentatious homes of Thomas Hardy and George Bernard Shaw as well as the suburban semi-detached house once owned by William Straw. All feature in the story of the First World War and its aftermath. So too does the ancient landscape around Stonehenge, the remote coastline at Orford Ness and the tranquil beauty of Sharpenhoe Clappers in the Chilterns. Early aviation was pioneered at Orford Ness, while bomber planes flew over Stonehenge after a night-bombing school was established nearby in 1917. More sombrely, Sharpenhoe Clappers was bought by the Trust with a gift from WA Robertson who wished to commemorate his two dead brothers. Robertson's generosity also allowed it to acquire Sutton House, Highcombe Edge and Dunstable Downs.

Many other properties came as a consequence of the war. Newark Park, for example, was bequeathed by the mother of James Clutterbuck, a young airman shot down by Manfred von Richthofen.

Along with the properties, of course, arrived a huge collection of material: photographs, paintings, documents and artefacts of every kind. At Dunham Massey, which had been the Stamford Military Hospital between 1917 and 1919, all sorts of objects had been hoarded away,

Left: From left to right: Harold, Hilda, Stephen and Robert Cawley. Harold was killed at Gallipoli in 1915, Stephen in France in the first weeks of the war. A third brother, Oswald, was killed in its last months. The Cawley family lived in Manchester and at Berrington Hall.

including an iron bedstead, wooden bedside table and drip stands; even a tin containing tubes of ointment for the treatment of patients burned by exposure to gas. These have all made it possible to re-create a ward in the drawing room at Dunham as it would have been during the war.

Dunham Massey is the centrepiece of the National Trust's First World War commemorations, but almost every property will have an echo of the conflict, in some cases muted, in others more distinct. Thanks to the dedication of staff and volunteers, stories are being uncovered all around the country, pieces adding to our understanding of the war.

Insights have come from the correspondence of Beale family members at Standen, or letters from the front line posted by Private Fred Hughes and Corporal Harold Hepworth which surfaced at Chirk Castle and Nostell Priory. They are not perhaps unique, but what is rare is to be able to visit a property from or to which letters were written and to find them much as they would have been one hundred years ago – or as at Lanhydrock House, to view the bedroom of Tommy Agar-Robartes almost as he left it in 1915, never to return. The National Trust links people to places, and through those places the lives of particular people are illuminated. They have not been forgotten.

1. HOME FRONT

On 4 August 1914, Caroline Kipling had a cold and noted in her diary that she felt unwell. Beside this comment her husband added, 'Incidentally, Armageddon begins today.' Rudyard Kipling was among the few to appreciate the enormity of what was to follow the outbreak of war. Not many shared his dark outlook. All across Europe borders were closing and armies mobilising. Excitement and celebration were everywhere.

BRITAIN·NEEDS

YOU·AT·ONCE

PUBLISHED BY THE PARLIAMENTARY RECRUITING COMMITTEE. LONDON. POSTER Nº 108.   PRINTED BY SPOTTISWOODE & Cº Lᵀᴰ LONDON. E.C.

The Kiplings were on holiday on the east coast of England at the time. Also holidaying on the Norfolk coast, near Cromer, was Clementine Churchill with her two children. Her husband, Winston, wrote to her there on 28 July in almost exultant mood. A man of invincible self-belief, he had a strong sense of destiny. The war offered opportunity to prove himself equal to his great ancestor, Marlborough. Its prospect allured him with a 'hideous fascination'.

Franz Ferdinand, heir to the Austro-Hungarian Empire, had been assassinated with his wife in Sarajevo on 26 June. Their assassins had been armed by the Serbs. As the two sides confronted one another, Germany supported

Left and right: By the autumn of 1915, fifty-four million posters had been distributed, some urging men to enlist, others encouraging people to invest in war bonds. These were sold to help fund the conflict. Taxes were also raised and money borrowed from abroad. With interest on the loans, by 1934 Britain owed the US over £800m – about £225bn at today's rates.

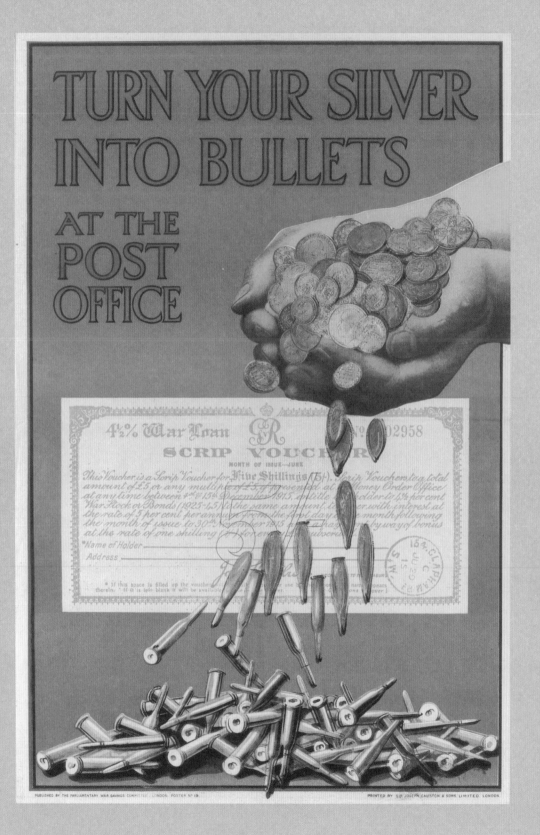

9

Austro-Hungary while Russia was allied to Serbia. And since Russia had a separate alliance with both France and Britain, and the latter two were tied by the Entente Cordiale, Britain looked like being drawn into war. When Germany invaded Belgium, the British government having pledged to defend Belgium neutrality, involvement became inevitable. At 11pm on 4 August, Winston, as First Lord of the Admiralty, commanded all ships to commence hostilities. The war had begun. Mobilisation papers were immediately sent out to army reservists and territorial soldiers. At Stourhead in Wiltshire, Sir Henry Hoare was requested to commandeer horses for the military. His estate diary for 4 August reads as follows:

'At 9.45 p.m. received Requisition of Emergency instructing me to buy Army horses... Wired Police Inspector, Sturminster Newton and Shaftesbury, to have everything ready at 7 and 8 a.m. on Wednesday August 5th. Starting from here 5.30 a.m. with Colonel Mansel and Mr Hoare, and got Emergency Orders signed by magistrates. Purchased 2 Chargers and 75 Yeomanry horses that day. Mr Caesar, my Sub-agent joined me at Gillingham to keep the books for the purpose of 75 Yeomanry horses. Finished up at 10.30, returned here and made our accounts for the day, finishing by 1.30.'

At Quarry Bank Mill the war was also to have an instant impact. According to company records, 'For a time after the opening of hostilities, business was completely paralysed. Short Time was immediately adopted as delivery of goods was brought to a standstill and stocks began to immediately accumulate. Liverpool market was closed for a week from the beginning of the war, and there was a rapid decline in values... Workpeople – especially men – began to leave as the prospect was not very promising and many vacancies occurred through men of military age having joined the army either as territorials or by voluntary enlistment.'

Everything was in turmoil. Stock Exchanges round the world crashed as insurance premiums rose, bond and stock prices tumbled due to investors seeking to liquidate their assets and exchange rates were volatile as cross-border creditors rushed to repatriate their money.

And across Europe, men were hurrying to enlist in their millions. In Britain, three-quarters of a million men joined the army in August and September alone. There were numerous reasons for this. Patriotism was clearly one motive, but for many it was a chance of adventure – an opportunity to escape the monotony of factory routine or the drudgery of life in the fields.

IF I ONCE
GET HOLD —

Joining up

On most of the large estates, employees were variously coerced or bribed into joining up. At Knole in Kent, men under fifty years of age were encouraged to volunteer. All did so, though this was not to everyone's liking. Lord and Lady Sackville did not live on amicable terms and while he may have been delighted by the loyal response of his staff, she was not pleased and wrote to Lord Kitchener to complain. She informed the Secretary of State for War, 'I think perhaps you do not realise, my dear Lord Kitchener, that we employ five carpenters and four painters and two blacksmiths and two footmen, and you are taking them all from us.'

Some firms, such as Shell, owned by Marcus Samuel of Upton House, made generous provision for their workforce. Marcus and his Board agreed that employees would 'be allowed to leave to join their colours, whether British or foreign, either compulsorily or voluntarily, that their posts be kept open for them, and that their salaries be paid for at least three months.'

These provisions reflect the fact that Shell was of its nature an international business. It had German subsidiaries and the statement was

Above: 1915 postcard depicting the Kaiser as a figure of fun. Rudyard Kipling took a less benign view. He wrote, 'The Hun is outside any humanity… Our concern with him is precisely the same as our concern with the germs of any malignant disease.'

Above: Castle Drogo under construction before the war. Within days of its outbreak twenty-nine men working on the site had enlisted. These comprised four stone cutters, five walling masons, one carpenter and nineteen labourers.

Right: Sir Marcus Samuel of Upton House, founder of the Shell Transport and Trading Company. He later became 1st Viscount Bearsted.

philosophical in suggesting that such employees would choose to fight for the enemy. It also presumed the war was to be brief. While Kitchener and others suspected otherwise, most people thought it would be over almost before it had begun; a review after three months seemed completely appropriate.

If some employees were encouraged to join the army, others were given little choice. At Castle Drogo in Devon, building work was interrupted by the war, owner Julius Drewe refusing to employ anyone of military age. This decision was communicated by Clerk of Works J.C. Walker who informed a colleague that 'we must get every single man to enlist between the ages of 19 & 35 … the wishes of Mr Drewe are that no man be employed on the job who should be in Lord Kitchener's army.'

On 19 September, Mr Walker wrote to A.J. Bennett, enclosing two weeks' wages, which came to £3. 4s. 0d, along with an additional 10/- to cover expenses. He also expressed the hope that 'you will have a good time doing your duty to your King and Country, as you did here. Then at the end of the War you will be able to come Home knowing that you, for one, have done your best to serve your Country in her hour of need. I trust you will come back safe when all is over unless you find that Army life suits you and you stop 21 years and finish as Colour Sergeant.' Sadly, this was not to be the case. Private A.J. Bennett was killed at Ploegsteert in Belgium the following May.

On the coast

Not everyone was full of rapture at the prospect of war. Writing to his wife, Margaret, on 3 August, Sydney Beale of Standen in Sussex was far from excited. He told her, 'I don't see how we can stay out and keep anything of our national honour.' The following day as war was declared, he wrote, 'There are some other husbands here who like me don't like it altogether, though I think we're already to go if the word comes. Meanwhile some of us keep cheery and one or two of us don't and get ragged greatly in consequence.'

Sydney was in Newhaven with the Sussex Regiment when war broke out and his letters give a sense of the activity around him. Rumours were incessant. On 4 August he told Margaret there were 'various tales flying about here, among others one that the Germans have fired on our ships in the North Sea.' Two days later, 'there have been three fellows arrested for spying – of whom two have been let go and one handed on to the police'. He'd also seen 'about three dozen Brighton motor buses' transporting 'ammunition for the guns in the fort' and taking away the 'practice stuff'.

Sydney was also naturally aware of shipping. Before this, on 3 August it looked as though 'The cross channel service has stopped here and the boats are lying at the quay and under orders to be ready at 2 hours' notice – if they are wanted it will be for the Expeditionary Force – expeditioning'. A week later, things had changed. 'The Expeditionary force has gone – at least 4 divisions out of the 6 due to go' while on 11 August, 'there are boats coming and going now frequently – lots of little tramps as well as the Cross Channel boats.' Sydney's resigned belief that entering the war was a question of honour was one shared by Frederick Hughes. Fred was a miner from North Wales who'd been brought up on the Chirk Castle estate. Writing to his brother Ted in June 1917 he said, 'I still disagree with you that this war could not (from our point of view) be prevented. In 1914 we were the same as we had always been, a peaceful loving nation, when up steps a nation in arms apparently against the world. What could we do? Stand still and watch with a clear conscience the atrocities committed on a small Country like Belgium by the Germans. No! We stepped in, not only to save the Belgiums, but to save our Honour which is more to us than anything.'

Ammunition shortages

As a territorial, Fred had arrived in France in November 1914. Already it was evident things were not going to plan. British factories were not yet geared up for war production and many experienced workers had enlisted, in turn causing a skills shortage. This was not a problem faced by the Germans who were formidably better supplied.

Alan Dawnay commented on the subject in a letter from France to his brother Guy, of Beningbrough Hall. On 22 September, he wrote, 'Day after day we are shelled more or less continuously with shrapnel & high explosive, day after day local attacks & counter attacks vary the monotony… The shell fire does very little harm … but all the same ten days of it becomes a trifle trying, though the men's spirits & nerves are standing the strain quite splendidly. What astonishes & bewilders the gunners is how the devil they get their ammunition … which seems to be unlimited!'

Below: Sydney Beale of Standen.

Things had not improved a few months later when Lieutenant William Armstrong of Cragside took part in the 2nd Battle of Ypres. In his account, *My First Week in Flanders*, he stated that 'the shortage of artillery ammunition was scandalous, and we received hardly any support from our artillery. The enemy's shells burst in hundreds all round and among us, and we could barely reply. The gunners were wringing their hands… Some people blamed the late Lord Kitchener, others the munition factories, and others again, the fact that the Dardanelles campaign had unexpectedly taken ammunition intended for the Western Front. But whoever was to blame, and whatever the causes, the fact remains that a great disaster nearly occurred for lack of shells.'

Lord Kitchener had been in charge of recruitment, munitions and military strategy, though many people doubted his ability to handle any one of the three areas with competence. By the time he drowned off the Orkneys when sailing for Russia in June 1916, he had already been relieved of responsibility for military strategy. He had also been severely criticised for the munitions crisis. One person who found him very much to blame was the former Viceroy of India, George Curzon of Kedleston Hall. He wrote to a friend, 'the papers and the public have got hold of the wrong end of the stick about K. "Genius for organization", "wonderful foresight" – alas, as we know only too well, the very things he had not got. His death came in a most fortunate hour for his reputation. For he will now always be a national hero.'

Kitchener is best remembered for the recruiting drive he led, and particularly the poster of him with peaked cap, moustache and imperious finger declaiming, 'Your Country Needs You'. Tens of thousands had answered his call, but tens of thousands had already been killed or wounded. The nation was running out of volunteers. The question of compulsory military service was becoming an issue.

Above: 1915 poster showing Lord Kitchener in recruiting mode. He was one of the few men to anticipate that the war would be long and costly.

Conscription

George Curzon had been advocating conscription since 1909 and in May 1915 wrote to *The Times* complaining that 'while our men were going through indescribable agonies in Flanders, there were at Manchester 30,000 looking on at 22 other men kicking a leathern ball about.' Most members of Herbert Asquith's cabinet were opposed to enforced recruitment, but casualty rates were draining the army fast.

A compromise solution was proposed by Lord Derby. Under his scheme, all men of military age would voluntarily register their name, agreeing in principle to serve if called upon to so. It was essentially compulsion, as Sam Beale wrote to his sister Helen, at Standen on 21 October 1915, 'Lord Derby's scheme strikes me as awfully good. As far as I can make out it is national service less the legal compulsion & … as it's called voluntary everybody is pleased as can be.'

Eventually the Derby Scheme was felt to be unworkable and once Churchill and David Lloyd George put their influence behind conscription, the Military Service Act became law in March 1916, despite Prime Minister Asquith's reluctance. While on active service on the Western Front, Winston Churchill had given an insider's account to William Croft, who in turn passed it on to his mother in a letter of January 1916. It seems Churchill 'described Asquith's position regarding compulsion as that of a cat being dragged by the tail across a slippery table. You know the sort of fight the cat puts up but she is compelled in spite of claws by "*force majeur*".'

From the outset of the war, men not in military uniform had been subject to taunts in public. Eventually many of those doing essential but non-military work were given identification. That same month, Dorothy Brown, Helen Beale's sister, had told her that her husband, Harold, had come home 'with a large and shining war badge on & a letter in his pocket from the Ministry of Munitions saying … that he should be exempted… Harold is very scoffing over it himself & says oh well it will postpone his going for a bit, but he thinks every blessed one will have left before very long.'

The Act obliged all single men between the ages of eighteen to forty-one to serve in the army, unless already in the Royal Navy, widowed with children, a minster of religion or working in a reserved occupation. In May that year this was expanded to include married men and in 1918 the upper age limit was extended to fifty-one.

Opposition to war

Sixteen thousand men resisted conscription and registered as conscientious objectors. They did so from a variety of motives. Some opposed the war on political or philosophical grounds; others because of their religious belief. Where right of conscience was recognised, alternative forms of non-military service were sanctioned. The Penrose family of Peckover House in Cambridgeshire were Quakers and all three of Lord Peckover's grandsons, Alexander, Lionel and Roland, served with the Friends' Ambulance Unit.

Opposition to war had been an integral part of Quaker faith for generations. It is a little harder to define the reason many members of the Bloomsbury Group refused military service, except perhaps that it was antithetical to their belief in individualism, creativity and pursuit of beauty. Some members, such as Virginia Woolf's husband, Leonard, and her friend Lytton Strachey were exempted on the grounds of ill-health.

Virginia's brother, Adrian Stephen, was the most ardent of Bloomsbury pacifists and defended others at their tribunals. Her sister Vanessa's husband, Clive Bell, wrote a pamphlet titled *Peace at Once*, published by the National Labour Press in spring 1915 but it was suppressed, while Vanessa's lover Duncan Grant and his lover David Garnett were conscientious objectors. They both agreed to become farm labourers as a form of acceptable war work and it was for this reason they all moved together to Charleston in Sussex, while Clive worked on a farm near Oxford.

Perhaps a more principled opponent of the war was Charles Trevelyan of Wallington near Morpeth. A radical Liberal MP from a family with a long history of liberalism, he nevertheless found himself estranged from his brother, parents and in-laws. In 1914 he'd been a minister at the Board of Education but resigned his government post, writing to his wife that, 'I was never clearer in all my life… We have gone to war from a sentimental attachment to the French and a hatred of Germany.'

Charles helped found the Union of Democratic Control (UDC) along with others such as the future Labour Prime Minister Ramsay MacDonald, philosopher Bertrand Russell and Liberal MP Philip Morrell. Philip Morrell's home at Garsington Manor (not National Trust) was where Clive Bell set to work as a farm labourer. It was to become a centre for opponents of the war including, in time, writers D.H. Lawrence and Siegfried Sassoon. Among other things, the UDC called for an end to secret diplomacy and peace terms that did not impose humiliating terms on the defeated nations. It was naturally castigated.

Below: Charles Trevelyan, of Wallington, viewed by his aristocratic neighbours as a class traitor because of his socialist views.

In an article in 1917, Charles Trevelyan wrote, 'the world war has revealed the real meaning of our social system. As imperialism, militarism and irresponsible wealth are everywhere trying to crush democracy today, so democracy must treat these forces without mercy. The root of all evil is economic privilege.' Not surprisingly, given his views, Charles joined the Labour Party in 1918. He was soundly beaten at the General Election that year, though he re-entered Parliament in 1922. He was detested by some of his aristocratic neighbours around Wallington who viewed him as a class traitor. His views on the war also remained sensitive and as late as 1931 the dragons on the lawn were on one occasion tipped over and on another tarred and feathered by a local army officer. Charles declined to press charges.

George Bernard Shaw

Probably the most outspoken critic of the war was Charles' friend, George Bernard Shaw. At its outbreak he had likened England and Germany to 'a couple of extremely quarrelsome dogs' and advised soldiers of both armies to 'SHOOT THEIR OFFICERS AND GO HOME'. He also argued that the 'conshy [conscientious objector] was the hero of the war and the man who would not enlist until he was forced was the coward'.

Despite the extreme nature of many statements, it wasn't entirely clear to people where Shaw really stood. He was a showman who delighted in paradox and liked to provoke controversy. But he was also, in his way, a patriot. He may have despised the war, but he did not wish to see Britain defeated and wrote that 'We shall have to fight and die and pay and suffer with the grim knowledge that we are sacrificing ourselves in an insane cause.'

Above: George Bernard Shaw (pictured here as a young man before the war) agreed with his friend Charles Trevelyan that the root of the war was economic inequality. He wrote, 'There are only two real flags in the world henceforth, the red flag of Democratic Socialism and the black flag of Capitalism.'

Right: The hydrogen gas that filled each Zeppelin was contained in 250,000 separate bags made from cows' intestines. Since the intestines were also used to make sausage skins for wurst, a type of sausage, a shortage developed and a law was passed in Germany forbidding people to make sausages.

If there were questions surrounding his real belief about the war, there was never any doubt about the sorrow he felt at the deaths of so many of his friends' sons. One of those was J.M. Barrie's foster son George Llewelyn Davies who, with his brothers, was the inspiration for Peter Pan and the Lost Boys. George was killed in March 1915. The son of the actress Stella Campbell, for whom Shaw created the role of Eliza Dolittle, was killed at the end of 1917. Writing to express his condolences, he scrawled, 'Oh damn, damn, damn, damn, damn, damn, damn, damn, DAMN, DAMN'. Shaw was a man adept at language, yet lost for words, the repeated monosyllable spoke more strongly than a thousand conventional commiserations.

The war was brought home to Shaw in October 1916 when a Zeppelin was shot down near Shaw's Corner in Hertfordshire. He had found the sight of it an awesome spectacle, and wrote to a friend, 'I positively caught myself hoping next night that there would be another raid' though watching the airship burn in the sky, he found himself curiously unmoved at the thought of 'its human contents roasting for some minutes (it was frightfully slow)'. He concluded, 'One is so pleased at having seen the show that the destruction of a dozen people or so in hideous terror and torment does not count… A pretty lot of animals we are!'.

Zeppelin raids!

Shaw's excitement at seeing the Zeppelin was echoed by others. The airships were obviously spectacular craft, all the more dramatic when illuminated by searchlights at night. Helen Beale's mother described one to her daughter, telling her 'there was a patch of white light in the shine thrown by search lights, & in the middle of it a tiny silver cigar slowly sailing north-west, & tiny orange light flashes going off at intervals.' The airships literally brought the war to the homes of people far from the front line and the remote threat of danger must have added to the thrill. At least in their correspondence, there is little trace of fear. Cis Dawnay was particularly keen to stress this when writing to her husband Guy, of Beningbrough Hall, 'No one here was in the least frightened, nor were they at all perturbed… '

Instead, the predominant emotion seems to have been one of exhilaration. In September 1915, Dorothy Brown told her sister Helen Beale, of Standen, 'We had great excitement the other night when the Zeps came over to London'. Cis wrote, 'We have just had a Genuine Zepp raid!!' Helen's mother informed her, 'I had the most extraordinary piece of luck … we saw a Zepplin. Think of that!' and William Croft's sister, Jan, wrote to their mother in October 1916, 'Fancy my luck seeing three burn in a month.'

Her delight was perhaps understandable. The Zeppelin had no bombing accuracy and the bombs fell indiscriminately, frequently killing children. Several had landed near Jan, but she reported, 'They were all dropped in almost the same spot as in the raid last Sept. and only did a little damage comparatively. No one killed or hurt. Our nursery six acres of glass full of tomatoes and grapes was flattened.'

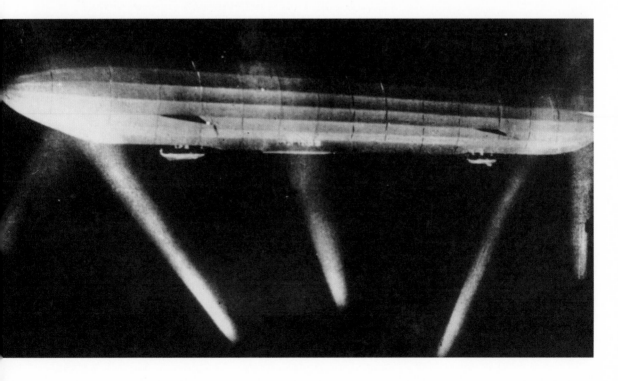

Like many other aspects of the war, the Zeppelin raids brought people together in a way perhaps unimaginable only a few years before. Servants and their employers bumped into one another on landings and seemed to share enjoyment of the drama together. Dorothy Brown told Helen, 'We had just retired to bed and were drowsing off when the maids came and knocked at the door saying that there was a horrid noise going on and that they thought it must be a Zepp, so out we had to get to find our 4 maids in very négligé attire on the landing outside our room.'

In her letter, Cis Dawnay let Guy know, 'I thought no time should be lost and hurried to the nursery only to meet my nursery-maid on the way who said she had seen the Zep & she saw the guns firing… I thought I ought to follow the Home Office's directions and take the children to the cellar … & carried them down to the housekeeper's room where we sat round the fire for half an hour. The gun fire only lasted for about 15 minutes… The night was wonderfully clear and my servants who were out were thrilled by seeing it.'

Some sort of propriety established itself in Jan's house, despite the confusion, 'I'd grabbed my clothes in a bundle and I and maids collided at

Above: Crashed Zeppelin, East Anglia. The soldiers beside the wreckage give a sense of the craft's huge size.

Opposite left: The imprint of a German airman, where his body had fallen to earth.

Opposite right: Crashed Zeppelin gondola.

top of stairs. Before we got half way down the bombs fell and house rocked. A. was putting on his clothes in his room and thought his ceiling was coming down and he came down in a hurry.

'Maids and I were putting on clothes in dining room, so we handed him a candle in drawing room! I was trying to pull on combinations while Lizzie would try to force me into a camisole! We were soon clothed and outside.'

A grim outcome was described in a letter from Jan to her mother in September 1916, 'Suddenly a bright light lit up the whole place – I thought they'd got the factory and expected to hear explosions – J. and I rushed round house and there was Zepp in flames!... It was soon flames all over and then only a red falling ball… Jack has been over to see it, it's about 6 miles away only a mass of wire and half melted aluminium and many bits of Germans, only two recognisable bits of what they think were engines and propellers – think of the height it must have fallen. There was a sort of hush when the flames burst out, and then one heard cheers from every direction – a perfect roar.'

About eighty Zeppelins flew on raids over Britain during the war years, of which thirty came down, destroyed either by British planes or mechanical problems. Although the initial attack had taken place in January 1915, it wasn't until June of that year that the first was shot down. This was largely due to the high altitude at which the Zeppelins flew, planes not having the capacity to reach them. The first to bring one down was Reginald Warneford of the Royal Naval Air Service. He was immediately awarded the Victoria Cross, though killed only ten days later.

Secret work at Orford Ness

Another pilot to destroy a Zeppelin was Frank Holder, stationed at Orford Ness in Suffolk. His plane was a slow but reliable FE2b, built by Ransome's agricultural engineers in Ipswich. He was accompanied by Sergeant Ashby as machine gunner. Frank described the encounter:

'Ashby and I finally took off at 1.55 a.m. on a perfect summer night with exceptional visibility. The Zeppelin was almost overhead and we had no difficulty in locating it and keeping it under observation… We reached our ceiling of 14,000 feet … only to find it still out of range but obviously losing height… As the airship continued to lose height … I altered course so that Ashby could use the easiest aim, firing straight ahead without deflection… Ashby, with a clear view of the target, fired three drums, the last at a range of about 300 yards, at which point we were aware of tracer bullets coming from the direction of the enemy. I started to take evasive action, but as we did so we saw flames appear at the point at which we were aiming. The time was 3.25 a.m.'

Below: Albert Ball was one of many combat pilots who spent a brief time at Orford Ness. His arrival was inauspicious, since he crashed on landing. The picture, taken during the winter of 1916–1917, shows him being led away from the craft in a wintry Suffolk landscape. When he died in France, in May 1917, he was Britain's leading air ace with forty four kills. He was twenty years old.

Orford Ness was one of just seven air-service stations when war broke out, though the number would rise to over three hundred by 1918. It was 2,000 acres of marsh, shingle and biting east winds. It was not hospitable, but its remote location had been chosen with purpose since the Ness was designed for experimental, often highly secret work.

By the end of the war over six hundred men were based on the site, including pilots, observers and scientists as well as members of the Chinese Labour Corps and German prisoners of war – the latter employed to build sea defences. The airmen were almost all specialist test pilots and from 1914 onwards they and the scientists collaborated on a range of research projects including the development of parachutes, self-sealing fuel tanks, interrupter gears, fire-proof clothing, photography, navigation and camouflage.

These are all things taken for granted now, but aeroplanes were still only just over ten years old and almost everything had to be improvised or pioneered. Sometimes researchers worked in conjunction with combat pilots who made suggestions or reported concerns. Occasionally, they were able to examine enemy aircraft and found, for example, that the Germans were far ahead in their development of self-sealing fuel tanks or the interrupter gear that synchronised machine-gun fire through propellers. Flying was inherently dangerous and much was done at the Ness to improve the reliability of navigation equipment so pilots could fly through cloud or at night when unable to chart their course using landmarks. Frank Holder also helped with the development of lighting for cockpit instruments, which along with the deployment of better runway flares, ensured that planes were better able to fly in the dark.

Stonehenge and night bombers

Such work was vital for pilots training on night bombers at a station hundreds of miles away at Stonehenge in Wiltshire. Flying had begun in the area as early as 1911 when the Committee for Imperial Defence recommended the creation of an Air Corps and a camp was established at Larkhill. Much early aviation development was carried out by a combination of entrepreneur showmen such as Samuel Cody, engineers like Charles Rolls and wealthy enthusiasts. The landing ground at Larkhill was closed, however, when huts were built in 1914 to accommodate 20,000 troops.

Many of the earliest planes had been relatively small and light monoplanes with a wingspan of 30 feet. By 1917 when the night-bombing school was established near Stonehenge the Handley Page bombers were twin engine bi-planes capable of carrying sixteen 112-pound bombs. Lieutenant Leslie Semple approved of the bombers. In his diary he said of them, 'These machines are excellent and the biggest yet. The top plane has a span of about 100 feet. Average speed 60 knots. Takes off very soon, fairly easy to land and

very strong undercarriage'. The planes' robust construction also gave the pilots marginally more chance of surviving a crash.

The Stonehenge area was not ideal for a flying school as the ground was mostly rough, undulating grassland, dotted with ancient burial mounds. According to Sergeant P.E. Butcher, a mechanic, 'One of the problems on the night flying ground took the form of two large barrows, said to be the mass burial sites of victims sacrificed on the Blood Stone at Stonehenge … many of our machines ran into them, but the War Office issued an order that on no account must they be moved so the accidents in the dark continued.'

One of the pilots affected was Leslie Semple. He recorded in his diary on 4 April 1918 that 'I was landing when my left wheel hit a large mound in the rough ground, instantly smashing one centre section strut and also swinging me round 90 degrees.' The following day he obviously had a difficult interview with Captain Oxland 'concerning the crashes I had had. I spoke out and assured him that it was no fault of mine. The airfield is in a rotten state and I have only had one crash previous to this in the whole of my flying career.'

Despite the problems, Leslie Semple seems to have appreciated the ancient monument at Stonehenge. Soon after his arrival at the camp he wrote, 'These stones are a great wonder... It must have required marvellous perseverance on the part of the Old Druids to bring these immense stones all this distance and pile them up in in the form of a place

Above: Aerial view of Stonehenge showing South Camp under demolition after the war. One of many ancient barrows is visible in the left foreground.

Right: South Camp under construction, 1917, divided by what later became the A303. The picture was taken from a Handley Page bomber.

of worship.' For Sergeant Butcher there were other 'added pleasures like flying over Salisbury and circling round the Cathedral spire.'

He had been posted to France within ten days of the war's outbreak and been twice decorated. An experienced engine fitter, it was men like him who kept the planes in the air and in his memoir he wrote he wished the reader was able to see the 'rigger's hands after he had been splicing, a difficult task, as was fabric stitching since the linen had to be made quite taut before doping. Seeing the finished job, one wondered how it was possible to do such work under difficult conditions.'

He was proud of the team who worked under him and felt 'it was a pleasure to serve under capable officers who took an interest in one.' As at Orford Ness, it was also necessary to use Prisoners of War at Stonehenge to help with the heavy work of wing folding and positioning. The demands on Sergeant Butcher and the other mechanics was constant as by the end of the war there were two separate camps, the aerodrome 'used by the day flying school until 7 p.m. and from then until 7 a.m. for night flying, so the sound of aircraft never ceased.'

On top of this, 'Being a training school there were plenty of crashes and forced landings all over the south of England as the pilots made their first night flights and cross country trips, and we had phone messages

STONEHENGE, SALISBURY PLAIN.

COPYRIGHT PHOTO., T.L.FULLER, AMESBURY.

from all over the place. How, and despite so many lads getting killed, for we were all living on our nerves, we managed to get the flying hours in, is still a mystery to me.'

One of the crashes was observed by Leslie Semple. What he found when he reached the scene was deeply distressing, 'Today about 2 p.m. saw a fellow spin into the ground on a DH9. Called up the ambulance and with another fellow ran with a fire extinguisher. On arrival found the pilot in a terrible condition, throat cut, eyes burnt out, bones broken, hair all burnt off – absolutely ghastly and still conscious. He was in terrible pain and asked to die. Gave address of his people etc., etc. Died at about 4 p.m.'

It is difficult to grasp how young these men were. On 11 June, a few days after witnessing the crash, Leslie noted in his diary, 'I am 19 years of age today. In my smaller diary I asked the question on 18th Feb "Where shall I be on my 19th birthday?" Well, I did not expect to be at Stonehenge.' Before the end of the month, his time there was complete. He noted on 26 June, 'Having finished the course here I obtained a clearance chit, returned all the stores I had drawn and paid my mess bill.' By 7 July, he was in France.

What he would have found there was described by 2nd Lieutenant Leslie Blacking who referred to himself as 'just a young fellow doing his best to perform what he was ordered to do. The lives of the two other crew, neither of whom could fly a plane, were in my hands, in addition to a

Above: Postcard of Stonehenge, looking west, with a plane and the outline of the hangar on the horizon to the left.

Left: Lieutenant Leslie Blacking. Of his time in France he wrote: 'I began to feel like what I was – a nineteen year old, a million miles from the exuberance of flying training back in peaceful England.'

Above: Handley Page bomber. It had been raised on a trestle so its compass could be calibrated.

ton of bombs. With no parachutes, although scared stiff, one had to keep calm… It had been one thing flying Handleys in training, just taking off and landing at Stonehenge… But this was to be the real thing taking off with a war load of bombs and bullets and fuel, battling along against the weather and the cold, the searchlights, ack-ack and Hun fighters.'

Birth of the RAF

Until the end of March 1918, all of the airmen and ground crew at Stonehenge would have been serving with either the Royal Flying Corps (RFC) or the Royal Naval Air Service (RNAS). This was because the army and navy had developed a separate flying capability. Responsibility for British air power was thus split between the RFC controlled by the War Office and the RNAS by the Admiralty. It inevitably led to problems.

Writing to Helen Beale of Standen from France in November 1916, her cousin Dick Bell Davies told her, 'We hear from home that our respected leaders have been indulging in a battle amongst themselves. A sort of three cornered duel between the Air Board, Admiralty and War Office. It will probably result in considerable changes in administration. If incidentally a few of our friends get pitched out of their offices into the Fleet or the trenches it will do some good.'

The night before the two services merged, Leslie Semple recorded, 'we all got drunk to celebrate the last night of the Royal Naval Service. Tomorrow the two air services … unite – for better or worse. Nobody is very pleased about it… In theory it is an excellent idea but it is very difficult to put into practice … because each service has its own traditions and the RNAS in particular prefers naval discipline and organisation, both undoubtedly being better than the military ditto.' Sergeant Butcher shared his gloominess, 'By what I could see this was the end of the RFC. Sure enough on 1st April it became the RAF and we were in a bigger muddle than ever, with the old RNAS amalgamated with us to form a single service.'

Marcus Samuel's company Shell supplied all of the aviation fuel used by the RFC and daily shipped 160,000 gallons of petrol to the allied armed forces. Without the commodity, the war would have been unsustainable and at least according to former Viceroy Lord George Curzon, 'the Allies floated to victory on a tide of oil.'

Since it was imported from many parts of the world, shipping losses were a constant problem, the distinctive shape of the tankers making them instantly identifiable to enemy submarines. One way round this problem was ingeniously solved by replacing the water ballast most cargo ships carried between the hold and the hull with oil. This was adopted by 1,280 vessels in June 1917, adding the equivalent capacity of one hundred tankers and allowing the importation of more than a million extra tons of liquid fuel into Britain.

Shortages, though, were a constant problem and Harold Brown wrote to Helen Beale on the subject in July 1916 saying, 'I was rather frightened over the petrol question, as to whether I should ever be able to get enough… I asked the authorities for just what I wanted which was 32 gallons a month and they gave me 12 which would last me for just about 10 days; however, a kindly garage man saved the situation for me, by getting me a supply, and I should get through all right. Also by adjusting the carburettor … I have managed to get the car doing as near 30 miles a gallon as doesn't matter.'

War production

As far as Shell was concerned, anyway, the war was good for business. Although the shipping fleet had been put at the disposal of the British government and losses of all kinds were incurred, Shell's profits nevertheless rose from £2 million in 1915 and 1916 to £3 million the following year and £4 million the year after that.

Things were less healthy for William Richard Morris, later Lord Nuffield of Nuffield Place, at his Cowley car factory in Oxford. Before war broke out he was selling one hundred cars a month but this fell to nine in August 1914 and eleven in September. A profit of £13,000 before the war became a loss of £1,000 for 1914 rising to one of £1,700 the following year. His problem was that cars were not manufactured at Cowley, merely

Left and right: Female workers at Cowley, Oxford. By the end of the war more than a million women were working in munitions factories.

assembled there using parts imported from America.

What saved the factory was an order for hand grenades, delivered in July 1915, followed by a contract to machine cases for the bombs fired from Stokes Trench Howitzers.

Morris's efficiency as a producer led to his appointment as a member on various committees controlling production of trench-warfare munitions. This in turn resulted in a request for him to produce mine sinkers. Large quantities of these were needed to lay in the North Sea minefield, the sinker being attached to the mine by a long length of wire hawser.

Since skilled labour was required for the manufacture of parts and to fit them together, it was initially estimated that only 40 could be produced each week. When Morris accepted the commission, he promised to supply 250 a week, sub-contracting work to various smaller producers. To ensure all parts were fully interchangeable, he had to provide these with special jigs and tools, some of which were made in Nottingham by firms whose machinery was normally used in the lace industry.

It took several months to establish this supply chain, but once in place the necessary components arrived in increasing quantities. These were then assembled by female labour at Cowley. By the war's end production was outstripping demand, Morris's factory producing 2,000 mine sinkers weighing half a ton each per week. Even so, he failed to make huge profits, finishing with a balance of £4,666. On top of this, once production ceased all government plant was removed, leaving Morris with pre-war machinery worn out after four years' continuous use.

Right: Male workers at the Cowley plant. Car manufacture continued at WRM Motors throughout the war, but with reduced sales. In 1919 it was re-named Morris Motors.

Machine guns in the park

In some ways the whole country was becoming worn down by the war. It had impinged on every aspect of daily life. At times it must have seemed as though every country house had been turned into a hospital, every piece of parkland dug with trenches for troop practice or turned over to agriculture. At Belton House in Lincolnshire a large area of the extensive parkland was given over to the newly formed Machine Gun Corps in 1915.

Machine guns were in short supply in 1914 since almost all of the General Staff were cavalrymen brought up on histories of classical warfare. They could see little role for the machine gun and had ordered only ten per year from Vickers from the early 1900s. When war broke out there were only two machine guns for each infantry battalion, in contrast with the Germans who possessed more than any other army in Europe. Their gunners were highly trained and, at regular inter-regimental competitions, winners received a watch inscribed with the Kaiser's name.

Trench warfare proved the deadly necessity of machine guns and a training ground was established at Belton House, along with another at nearby Harrowby. The ground at Belton House was like a satellite town on the edge of Grantham, complete with its own sewage works, electricity and railway station. Troops lived in huts with corrugated iron roofs and

Below: YMCA hut, Belton Park.

Right: Poster, Belton Park. Belton Park had been used for troop-training purposes for many years before the war, but only with temporary encampments. The Machine Gun Corps camp established in 1915 was more like a small town, but was completely demolished in 1922 when the MCG left.

Y.M.C.A. No. 2 Hut, Belton Park.

asbestos walls and were fed by twelve cook houses each
serving a thousand men. Along with all this, there were a
couple of churches and a YMCA. By the time it closed in
1922, 170,000 men had passed through the camp. Twelve
thousand were to be killed in action.

The course lasted six intensive weeks, with gunners
firing around a million rounds a week. Some, like
Frederick Hunt, had previously trained at Harrowby. In
his memoir he said it had 'involved handling, dismantling
and maintaining machine guns – even when blindfolded –
to simulate night-time conditions at the front. Long hours
were spent on theory and practice in map reading,
deployment of guns in attack and defence, and to qualify
on all types of guns – even enemy weapons in case they
were usable after capture.'

From there he transferred to Belton where his company
'was a cosmopolitan crew of some two hundred men… We
used animal transport: there were six horses for officers'
use, eight mules and eight limber wagons for guns,
ammunition and equipment. The company moved out of
Belton one cold morning before dawn. As we marched
through Grantham's main street to the railway station it

Don't be Alarmed!
the BELTON BOYS.
are "On Guard."

was apparent that our movement was not all that secret. A number of local women
volunteers had set up gas boilers and trestle tables … and all ranks paused to drink a
welcome cup of hot tea. Mine was handed to me by Lady Brownlow, the aged and
dignified lady of Belton House.'

Hard times

If at times it must have appeared as if the whole country had become a vast military camp,
it might also have seemed that everyone was subject to army discipline. In August 1914
the 'Intoxicating Liquor (Temporary Restriction) Act' was introduced, curtailing
drinking hours to a maximum of six per day with a compulsory afternoon break.

The rationing of sugar was introduced in January 1918 with regulations concerning
the manufacture of sweets and jam. By April, meat, butter, cheese and margarine had also
been added to the ration list. Britons were forced to have two meatless days a week and
when food was available it was often of poor quality – from October 1917 bakers had been
allowed to add potato flour to bread.

Much of the food crisis was due to loss of cargo ships by U-boat activity. In April 1917
alone, Britain lost over 800,000 tons of shipping. The Home and Colonial Stores
assessment was bleak, 'In view of the Government having commandeered Cheese, and
now Butter, the activities of enemy submarines, and the prevailing high prices, the outlook
for the future as regards both Volume and Profit is causing us very great anxiety.

THE HOME AND COLONIAL STORES LIMITED

HEAD OFFICES:
2 & 4 PAUL STREET, LONDON, E.C.

5th August, 1914.

TO THE PUBLIC:

The Directors are anxious to minimise the hardship on the working Classes which will be caused by a further rise in the selling prices of Food Stuffs, and with that object have decided not to advance present prices so long as that course can be avoided, and they appeal to the general body of their customers to co-operate with the Directors by restricting their purchases to normal requirements.

To guard so far as they can against advantage being taken of this decision and the consequent depletion of the Company's Stocks before the week-end when the purchases of the Working Classes are chiefly made the Directors have decided to close their Branches to the public throughout the country on **MONDAYS** and **THURSDAYS** until further notice.

BY ORDER.

Above: The war began with fears about food shortages and ended with restrictions and rationing. Home and Colonial Stores poster on food pricing, from Castle Drogo. Julius Drewe owned the stores and used the wealth it provided to fund construction of the castle.

There was an under-supply of coal as well as food, so winters were a misery. The introduction of Day Light Saving in 1917 was resented, and at Quarry Bank Mill it was felt to be uneconomic, where it was stated on 9 April, 'Changed on to summer time. The date is certainly too early. Lighting up in the morning had ceased for about 10 days, but had to be resumed. After such an exceptionally long and dark winter this was very annoying to everybody concerned beside involving an additional use of gas.'

The Defence of the Realm Act (1914) had added all kinds of restrictions such as making it an offence to loiter under a bridge or whistle for a taxi after 10 p.m., while government advisers and busybodies were everywhere. Rudyard Kipling complained, 'I find in these days one can only just keep abreast of the daily detail of living as laid down for country people by Agricultural Departments, Barnyard Brigadiers and all the other time-wasting, work-killing Jacks and Jades in office who have been let loose upon us!'

Unrest was widespread. Early in 1918, food protests were planned in Burwash and Kipling was deeply concerned because the prime agitator was a woman previously employed at Bateman's as a servant. He feared she would lead a mob to the house and incite violence, though it seems she never did.

Strikes were another issue throughout the conflict and in September 1915 Harold Brown wrote a furious commentary to Helen Beale, telling her, 'It fairly makes one's blood boil to think what damage those skunks are doing to the common cause … shooting seems too good for men who can behave as a lot of these workmen are evidently doing. I wish the Germans would send a Zeppelin or two to South Wales and one or two other parts of the country to drop bombs upon some of the strikers. It might perhaps remind them that England is at war.'

On top of everything else, the war was costing the country a fortune, expenditure running at £6 million per day in 1918. It was a colossal sum paid for by hugely increased taxation and massive borrowing. Even children were contributing to the war effort. In April 1915 the Log Book of Stourhead School, Stourton, Wiltshire, recorded that 'During the past six weeks the children have subscribed the sum of One Pound Nine Shillings. The money will be spent in providing necessaries for Stourton Soldiers engaged in the War. One sailor and one prisoner in Holland.'

More than two years later the Stourton men were still fighting and its end seemed no nearer. Some had begun to fear the war would last forever, or at least until every young man had been killed.

Sanctuary

One man who knew as much of the war as most was the poet Siegfried Sassoon. He had enlisted in 1914, been awarded the Military Cross, made a public declaration against the conduct of the war believing it possible to negotiate an honourable peace, been treated for shellshock at Craiglockhart Hospital in Edinburgh, returned to the front line, been wounded and finally discharged. His younger brother and best friend had both been killed. Towards the end of 1918, he paid a visit to Lindisfarne Castle in Northumberland. In his autobiography he recalled:

'After driving across the wet sands to the island at low tide, we spent the afternoon with the only occupant of the castle. This was none other than Madame Suggia, who enchanted us with her immense vitality and charm. It needs no saying that Suggia on the concert platform has been the loveliest and most romantic of virtuosos…. How then can one find words to describe her playing of a suite by Bach in the reverberant chamber of a lonely and historic castle…? This was an experience which I will always remember with gratitude… For it was the first time I felt completely remote and absolved from the deadly constraints of war.'

With his friend Wilfred Owen, Siegfried was perhaps the greatest poet of a war defined by poets. In 1914, Laurence Binyon visited Pentire Head where he wrote *For the Fallen*.

They shall grow not old, as we that are left grow old:
Age shall not weary them, nor the years condemn.
At the going down of the sun and in the morning
We will remember them.

He could not have known how many would have to be remembered when the war finally came to an end four gruelling years later.

2. WOMEN AT WAR

For every man that was killed, many others were injured. Over the course of the war, more than two million British and Empire soldiers were wounded. That huge number meant that existing hospitals were overwhelmed and from the outset larger houses in town and country were offered as hospital accommodation. Clandon Park, Cliveden, Attingham Park, Polesden Lacey, Overbeck's, Dunham Massey… the list appears endless.

Belgian refugees began arriving at Clandon and Attingham Parks in October 1914 following the fall of Antwerp. Many were badly injured and in some cases hadn't eaten for more than two days. Attingham Park opened with only eleven beds on 20 October but these were expanded to fifty in 1917 and by April 1918 had risen further to sixty beds. Clandon at that early stage of the war could take one hundred patients, one of whom was to die on arrival and another just a few days later.

Hospitals such as those at Clandon and Attingham were staffed by a mixture of trained professionals and volunteers. Sometimes the organisation was administered by a qualified doctor, but very often it was in the charge of the lady of the house. Almost by definition, since they were unpaid, the voluntary nurses tended to come from relatively prosperous backgrounds, though their lack of training meant that they were at first restricted to the most menial tasks.

Above: *The Sisters*, by Edmund Dulac, 1917. Three women stand hand in hand, representing members of the Land Army, nurses, and munitions workers. Of the three options, nursing was considered most socially desirable for women from genteel families.

Life on the wards

This was the situation faced by Margaret Van Straubenzee when she arrived to work as a Voluntary Aid Detachment (VAD) nurse at Clandon Park, Surrey, in October 1916. Her initial duties required her to wash the marble floors, 'take round the meals and wash up; get the staff's tea ready at 9.30 a.m.; take round "specials" to the patients at 10 a.m.; clean all the forks, spoons, & brasses; and help in the ward to make beds in the afternoon or evening.'

Margaret also had to deal with some distressing cases almost from the outset. 'Several of the wounded had an arm or a leg blown off, and there was one case with both legs and one arm missing... Operations were going on day and night. There were frequent haemorrhages; on one occasion I had to hold the stump of a leg for quite a long time, when the first dressing (after the amputation) had to be done, and a horrible sight it was.'

Death was part of her routine and she 'often had to deal with dying men, but the orderlies always "laid them out", and we had only to disinfect the bed and locker and put them ready for the next case.' Even so, it must have been grim work.

Above: The Marble Hall, Clandon Park. A forty-foot square cube with stuccoed ceiling and elaborate carved fireplace, the eighteenth century entrance hall must have been seemed a strange place to recuperate after the horror of trench warfare.

For young women who had previously been ladies of leisure, the schedule was also demanding with occasional half-days off but only one full day's leave a month, on which Margaret and friends had some 'delightful expeditions … when we bicycled all through the lovely Surrey villages and lanes.'

Clandon Park was an 'Other Ranks' hospital, meaning that few of the men would have been of her own social standing. This was another aspect of Margaret's education, for in common with most VADs she was probably meeting working-class men for the first time who were not servants or another form of hireling. Generally everybody seems to have got on well. The patients were grateful for the care they received and the nurses felt instinctive compassion for the wounded soldiers; formerly rigid boundaries were dissolved by shared humanity.

While some of the nurses may have come from aristocratic families, Clandon Park itself was old and splendid enough to entertain a couple of ghosts. One of these was supposedly that of a former Countess of Onslow who was said to walk through the ballroom in a green dress and vanish beyond a locked door into the hunting room.

Margaret remembered, 'several patients asked me who the pretty old-fashioned lady was "who walked through the ward last night and disappeared through the door?"' It seems these questions were nearly always asked by patients who had only just arrived by convoy, though Margaret never saw the apparition herself. Neither did she hear the sound of ghostly hooves galloping to the front door, though one of her colleagues claimed to have done so.

When the house was converted into a hospital, Lord Onslow's dressing room became an operating theatre as it had a running water supply and

Below left: Page from autograph book belonging to Amy Bates, who nursed at Clandon Park.

Below: Patients at Clandon Park. One man treated at Clandon after Gallipoli was returned to active service. Wounded again, on the Western Front in the autumn of 1917, he found himself back in the same ward, adjacent to the bed he had previously occupied.

'S' awfully 'S Nice..

With my best wishes & good luck to Nurse Bates.

Wounded at Ypres Dec 2nd 1917.

Rfm L Month 4th Batt Rifle Brigade

reliable north-east light. Conditions were slightly more difficult at Dunham Massey in Cheshire, the operating theatre being at the bottom of the stairs, but placed there because it was by a little toilet provided with running water installed for the convenience of men using the adjacent billiard room. Lack of much natural daylight meant that some procedures had to be carried out with a nurse holding a torch, by which the visiting surgeon from Manchester had to work.

Being on a much larger scale, Clandon Park had more space for beds, some of which were in the very grand entrance hall (see the photograph on page 37). At Dunham Massey the main ward was in the drawing room, which had been cleared for the purpose. If it is likely that few VADs had ever had much to do with men from the lower classes, it is equally true that few of the men would have ever found themselves in such opulent surroundings – other than as a servant.

Clandon Park was a 'Primary Hospital', which meant it received patients direct from ports of disembarkation, the wounded often with their original field dressings and occasionally still plastered with mud. After the first influx of Belgian refugees had been treated and dispersed, there were periods when the hospital was quiet. This was not to last and as the war intensified, pressure for beds increased, at which time Lady Onslow was appointed Commandant in Charge.

In September 1915 men began to come in from the Battle of Loos and not long after that a convoy arrived from the Dardanelles (north-west Turkey). The latter were haggard, many wracked with typhoid and dysentery, and twenty were dangerously ill, though all but one recovered.

After January 1916 the operating theatre was in continuous use and around seven hundred operations were performed. Almost all were direct from the front line. From October 1914 until it closed in April 1919, 5,059 patients were treated, although in 1919 some 151 of these were suffering with Spanish influenza – Margaret Van Straubenzee herself becoming a patient in the hospital in which she had worked for so many years.

Inevitably there were deaths. Some were buried in the local churchyard, but wherever possible the bodies of those who died were returned to their native town. Some, like Archibald Gunn of Queensland, Australia, and Private Curtis and Able Seaman Davis, both Canadians, were far from home. Another North American, Private 252912 C.R. Russell died at Cliveden, Buckinghamshire, on Armistice Day. He is buried in plot 31 in the secluded Italian Garden given over to interments.

Egypt

Women like the Countess of Onslow of Clandon Park were bred on imperious lines. It probably never occurred to her that what she asked for would not materialise. Margherita Howard de Walden of Chirk Castle was not quite of the same pedigree, but she had an equally determined personality. So when she received a cable suggesting that if she were 'prepared for difficulties and opposition' she should 'bring out hospital and stores and equipment and nurses as soon as possible', she responded instantly, although leaving two small children behind. 'Out' was to Alexandria, in Egypt.

Margherita may have been motivated by the fact that her husband, Lord Howard de Walden, known as Tommy, was with the army at Gallipoli and she wished to be near him. That he was one of the richest men in the world meant she could comfortably afford to furnish a hospital. Having made up her mind, she then went to 'call on Tommy's old friend the Matron of the Metropolitan Hospital' who was 'enthusiastic and a tremendous help'.

Nurses were secured and then 'one ordered hundreds of jolly-coloured striped pyjamas. Jams and chocolate, stores, and medical stores, instruments, blankets, sheets, etc. and foodstuffs and much more besides.' Once provisioned, she then booked passages for 'eleven nurses, a cook and maid with thirty-six cases on a P.&O. ship' – and set sail for Alexandria.

It was not long before there was an inrush of patients after the Suvla Bay landings at Gallipoli at the beginning of August 1915. 'Casualties absolutely poured in. They unloaded them on to the quays where vans and lorries picked them up … some had an hour or several hours lying unattended with the blazing sun tearing their nerves. So many wounded had developed gangrene on the voyage over, with a shortage of nurses and frequently no one at all to change dressings.' It seems it was left to frail Lady Caernavon to provide sunshade and organise cups of hot tea to cool in order to give the poor men some respite.

At that early stage the hospital was restricted in the type of patients it could accept, since for much of the time it didn't have a doctor. On one occasion a young soldier with a bullet wound in the chest was accidentally admitted. The nurses said he had to be operated on, but nursing etiquette obliged them not to do it themselves. They persuaded Margherita to undertake the operation, with their instruction, so 'I was told which sterilized scalpel to use and how to make the incision, and to make it long enough and deep enough, and then was given forceps with which to hold back the skin. They helped with squeezing the bullet out, and cleaning the wound, and then handed me threaded and sterilized surgical needles and told me how to sew it up and tie the gut.'

Although immensely wealthy, Margherita was definitely not

My darling John. How I wish I could come & pull
crackers with you & Babins Rabbit on xmas day.
I know you will have a lovely time & be
ever so happy. I will be thinking of you all
& playing with my soldier boys. You see then

42

squeamish. Nor was she afraid to take on the humblest tasks. On one occasion, all of the servants having left without word, she found there was no one to clean the toilets. And 'because I could not ask anyone else to do so' she 'washed out and disinfected the dysentery lavatories and wash-rooms' herself.

Over the next few months her hospital was able to take in two hundred patients, but in May 1916 she returned home on leave with her husband, the only woman on the troopship. And on becoming pregnant with their fourth child, she did not return to Egypt, while he was destined for the Western Front. She had done her bit.

Italy

Another who did her bit was Teresa Hulton. Teresa, who later became Lady Berwick and lived at Attingham Park, was brought up in Italy which entered the war on the Allied side in 1915. Once hostilities commenced, a set of redoubtable ladies decided to provide help to the Italian wounded, despite not speaking the language. Isabel Campbell approached Teresa, then aged twenty-five, on behalf of the group. Her letter of 30 September

Opposite: Letter to her four-year old son John, from Margherita Howard de Walden of Chirk Castle. Sent at Christmas, 1915.

Left: Teresa Hulton, later Lady Berwick of Attingham Park, Shropshire.

43

Above: Behind the wheel; Teresa Hulton in Italy. The war gave independence and opportunities to women unimaginable only a few years before.

opened in typically forthright style,

'Dear Miss Hulton, I suppose you don't by chance want a job do you? Tilly Cox told me she thought that perhaps you might be doing nothing.'

She went on to invite Teresa to work in a chalet that hadn't yet been built and wondered 'if you would care to come and help us, as our Italian is most rudimentary, and yours would be quite invaluable.' Teresa obviously replied encouragingly to this overture and on 12 October a second letter arrived. It gave a little more information about the accommodation, which 'had no luxuries of any sort, such as hot water, and other discomforts the nature of which you can guess.'

She continued, 'We also have daily air raids, generally one for breakfast and another for tea, and two bombs have been dropped not far from our little chalet. But I don't suppose that worries you.' She ends by repeating her assertion that 'it would be very nice if you came, as neither of us can speak Italian, and you would be fearfully useful.' Teresa was evidently not put off, by Isabel's abrupt manner or the lack of hot water, or even by the twice daily bombs. She accepted, and took her sister, Gioconda, with her.

They were housed in a chalet near the front line where they fed and tended the wounded, administered first aid and assisted the doctor. In six months they treated 50,000 wounded men, an average of nearly 300 per day – and in July 1917 they tended 1,600 men within twenty-four hours.

Rivalries and romances

Close to the reality of war, Teresa presumably had little time for social pettiness. Further from the front line, trivial matters could become contests of will. Ben Mitchell, a patient in the Mere Hospital near Stourhead, Wiltshire witnessed such a struggle between Alda, Lady Hoare of Stourhead and Mrs Troyte-Bullock, both visiting dignitaries.

Ben recalled that Lady Hoare visited the hospital one day and gave each of the patients five Woodbine cigarettes. Learning of this, Mrs Troyte-Bullock responded by giving them ten when she next called. Lady Hoare then retaliated by giving each man ten Players, to which Mrs Troyte-Bullock thrust back with twenty. This was a gesture Lady Hoare declined to equal, greatly to the patients' disappointment. Ben also claimed Mrs Troyte-Bullock served better teas, as it was more plentiful at Zeals House. He suspected his host was obtaining it on the black market.

Although there wasn't a hospital at Stourhead, Lady Hoare frequently had patients from Mere to visit. On one occasion she had taken some of the men to view the stables where a stallion was just about to mount a mare. In Ben's account the horse was 'having rather a difficult job and so Lady Hoare put on this velvet gauntlet glove and helped the stallion. We were terribly embarrassed, but she didn't take the slightest bit of notice and said, "I've done that very often."' It is not known whether Mrs Troyte-Bullock chose to follow suit.

Many of the smaller hospitals were for convalescent patients rather than those more seriously wounded. Polesden Lacey in Surrey was one and Sharpitor, or Overbeck's, in Devon, another. On the south-west coast, the hospital at Sharpitor was opened in April 1915, in memory of the Verekers' son, Robert, who'd been killed in the earliest days of the war. The house was given rent free and many local people made contributions of food and gifts and arranged outings for the inmates. George Vereker also did much to entertain them, putting on shows, billiards, picnics, whist drives and shooting competitions.

Like Clandon Park it was for ordinary soldiers rather than officers. And since it was for convalescence only, they travelled from Exeter and Newton Abbot where they had received primary care. Most men stayed for two to three months and, at its busiest, Sharpitor could accommodate fifty-four men. Seven out of every ten men were returned to active service and by the time of its closure in January 1919, 1,020 men had been cared for.

As at many such places, one of the nurses kept an autograph book in which patients could draw pictures, or leave messages or poems. One man, signing himself 'Shrapnel Jack' wrote,

Man's inhumanity to man
Makes countless thousands mourn.

The more I see of man
The more I like my dog.

It was a convivial place and must have been conducive to romance since fifteen of the patients got married to local women, three of the Tommies marrying nurses. The final Christmas in 1918 was celebrated 'in true Yuletide fashion' and it was reported in the local paper that, 'commencing at 7 a.m., Father Christmas went round with full stockings' and that 'at breakfast the men found their presents all laid out'. The paper added that through 'the kindness of many donors the dinner was sumptuous, roast turkeys, roast goose and plum pudding, heaped up dishes of fruit, sweets, etc. and the tables covered with crackers'. Games were played and prizes bestowed. It seems that when the hospital closed at last, tears were shed when staff, nurses, patients and orderlies linked arms for a rendition of 'Auld Lang Syne'.

Christmas at Sharpitor resembled those at Clandon Park as reported by nurse Margaret Van Straubenzee who wrote that 'We spent a very jolly Christmas in 1916, and some of the talented members of the staff got up a concert to entertain the patients. The Countess of Onslow and her Secretary sang and acted the duet *Madam, will you walk, Madam, will you talk, etc*" which was also much appreciated.'

Below: The Great Hall at Dunham Massey was converted to a ward with twenty-five beds.

Right: Convalescents in the inner courtyard, Dunham Massey. The Countess of Stamford's daughter, Lady Jane, is sitting on the steps, left.

Sister Bennett's log

The Stamford Military Hospital at Dunham Massey was overseen by Lady
Stamford, but its day-to-day running was in the charge of Sister Catherine
Bennett. She was evidently a highly efficient woman and at the end of the
war presented Lord Stamford with a complete record of all the patients
who had stayed at the hospital between its inception in April 1917 and its
closure in February 1919. She detailed not merely the patient's name and
regiment, but the dates of admission and discharge, type of wound and
course of treatment.

Not surprisingly, given the nature of trench warfare and concentration
of high explosives and machine-guns, the two largest categories of injuries
were 33 per cent admitted with shrapnel or bomb wounds and 22.4 per
cent with rifle or machine gun wounds. Eight per cent had been gassed
and another 8 per cent were suffering fractures. Of the remainder, many
were non-combat cases such as arthritis and pneumonia, though these may
have been exacerbated by conditions in trenches. A few, such as a case of
ingrowing toenails, appear to be non-military in origin. Four patients were
admitted to Dunham Massey with shellshock, three with trench fever and
five with trench feet. Of these latter eight, six were admitted between 15
and 25 January 1918, which probably reflects terrible winter conditions.

Phyllis Brandon *Catherine Bennett.* *Self.*

Altogether there were forty amputations at the hospital.

A fairly typical case, if one existed, was Private J. Hill who had '1st finger of R. hand' amputated. 'The whole hand was in a very septic condition, two further operations were performed in June for the removal of necrosed bone, & unhealthy tissue… Amputation of the limb was considered advisable, but Dr Cooper saved it, at patient's special request.'

One poignant instance was that of Private Harvey, admitted a month before the war ended with a bullet wound to the chest and shellshock. 'The patient stammered very badly. Miss Shirley, VAD, gave him lessons & exercises which greatly helped him, before leaving the patient could speak almost normally. He was discharged to duty.' Fortunately for him, by the time Private Harvey was released the war was at an end.

Nursing on the Western Front

As a VAD nurse Miss Shirley, like Margaret Van Straubenzee, would not have been fully qualified and in an earlier time much of her work would have been considered degrading for a person of polite background. Another young woman in that situation was Margaret Greg, of Quarry

Above: Lady Jane Grey (pictured right). Later in life she described helping at an operation, 'I saw the brain… pulsating, which interested me enormously. I held the torch in front and saw the bullet being extracted by the surgeon.'

Right: Jolly boating weather for nurses and patients at Morden Hall Park. When not in bed, patients wore blue uniforms to distinguish them from soldiers on the active list.

Bank Mill, not far from Dunham Massey. She had joined the Cheshire Detachment towards the end of 1914 or early the following year with a contract for '6 months or until not wanted'. After a short period of preliminary training she was sent to the Rest Station at Boulogne. This station must have been a shock for a young woman used to a comfortable life, comprising eight luggage vans in a siding for use as kitchen, dispensary, stores, staff room, reserve store, workshop and orderlies' room. Much was improvised with tables and cupboards made from packing cases and mugs from condensed-milk tins. The old granary where she lived was similarly furnished.

In the middle of March 1915, only a short time after her arrival in France, the Battle of Neuve Chappelle began and the Rest Station handled almost 2,000 of the 15,000 men either killed or wounded in the action. The injured arrived in cattle-trucks and it was up to the nurses to change the field dressings that had been applied and provide tea and cheer.

From Boulogne, Margaret moved to Abbeville where the hospital was a 'wooden table in a great draughty goods shed with a little enclosure of droopy canvas', though in her diary on 30 April she recorded that all set to work to make the 'so-called dressing station a bit more like such'. Then in May she had a 'wire from Glazebrook that Arthur is wounded and at No 7 St Hosp [Stationary Hospital]'. She was given a pass to visit her brother and was 'with A from 4.45 to 5.30 p.m. he could not speak being hit in the jaw, but wrote, he has had a bad time on Hill 60 & no sleep the last three weeks.' Arthur recovered but was later to be killed while flying with the Royal Flying Corps in 1917.

Margaret nursed through the battles of Loos and the Somme, during which time she was Quarter Master in addition to her other duties. Her diary records that the allowance per thousand men was '17lbs of Cocoa or 7lbs of Tea, 50 Tins of Condensed Milk, 30lbs of sugar, 2 loaves to each 8 men and 125 Tins of Jam'.

She had a brief spell back in England but returned to France in March 1918, and was stationed near Dunkirk. Her arrival coincided with the start of the German offensive and on 26 March she wrote, 'Air raid last night, no dug-outs, shrapnel fell like rain in the garden, battery behind kicks up quite a din.' Her younger brother, Robert, was killed in May and she found 'everyone was sympathetic but so busy not given time off.'

The situation remained tense. In June she records, 'awful night, no lights, heaps of shrap, bombs pretty close, 2 or 3 found dead before getting into ward – Surgeon Welland back from leave, operated all night – pitiable night – tin-hat useful going to and from wards.' She continued in France until the end of the war and on returning to England trained to be a doctor with a special interest in orthopaedics.

Below: Nurse Margaret Greg, who came from Quarry Bank Mill. On June 2 1915 she helped with a 'head case', an amputee and 'a gassed mad Scot's Greys man.' In her diary next day she recorded, 'the head case died, the amputation may do so… & he is a sweet boy of 18. My mad man… is to go home tonight.'

Right: Nurses on the lawn at Standen, Sussex. Among them is Helen Beale's sister, Maggie.

VAD training

Although not known to one another, Helen Beale of Standen was also a VAD nurse in France for much of the first two years of the war. She had been brought up in a socially privileged family and exclusively educated. When she went to London for basic training, her letters sound as if written from boarding school. One of them in September began, 'Thank you first ever so for the chocs. – they are scrumptious.' More sombrely, a few paragraphs later she adds of her work,

'It is most interesting and Matron and the Staff Nurse are very kind and nice. I must say though that the first morning was rather trying – you felt such a gooby not knowing where or how anything was to be done – and so in the way. The first thing was to go and watch dressings being done, and when it came to a big hip one where the poor chap was being horribly hurt,

*I turned green – or felt it – and went to have some fresh air!…
today I have been in at an operation for pyaemia on a tiny
and wasted baby that they thought very likely wouldn't live…
There is an appendix tomorrow… A rather grisly letter but I
feel so immersed in it I can think of nothing else!'*

After only a few months she was shipped to France. In the diary she
briefly kept, Helen noted on arrival that the 'atmosphere is distinctly
chilling; I say we are made to feel rather like pariahs and it is obvious we
are not to forget we are VADs… In the ward it is alright though, I am
merely treated as rather an ineffectual housemaid at present, and I do help
with the dressings now and then.' Things changed once the volunteer
nurses showed their capabilities and she later told her mother, 'though the
atmosphere suggests that we are somewhat interlopers – at meals and so on
– I think it is thawing … in my ward they are very pleasant and I think
appreciative of my efforts.'

Helen obviously embraced the demands of France, feeling that in some ways she was sharing a small part of the hardships suffered by the men she cared for. Once her first period of six months' duty was at an end, she had to decide whether or not to sign up again. She chose to on the grounds that 'I can't help all the time feeling that it's a bit faint hearted not to go on when one has the opportunity of being treated just like they treat the male thing; it seems a bit weak somehow to give up and want more holiday and a change when they don't get it or get the chance of it.'

Below: Helen Beale of Standen in WRNS uniform. She inspired intense loyalty in her subordinates, many referring to her as 'Wren Mother'.

Off to join the WRNS

Helen Beale nursed in France through the Somme battle, but came to feel she could make a bigger contribution in other areas, wanting to 'channel where one's abilities can give most in service to the country.' She thus transferred to the Women's Royal Naval Service.

Another woman to have served first in France and then move to the WRNS was Matilda Talbot of Lacock Abbey. The women they served with took on a multiplicity of roles, including as drivers, cooks, typists, clerks and domestic workers. In her memoir, *My Life and Lacock Abbey*, Matilda said 'Some worked in the wireless section, some at "deleting crashes" which meant sorting out the usable parts from a crashed aeroplane… By degrees the girls took up almost all the jobs the men had previously done.'

Helen was clearly an excellent organiser, finishing the war as a Divisional Director. She also inspired great loyalty in her colleagues. Many wrote, referring to her as 'Wren Mother'. One particularly effusive offering has the quality of a schoolgirl crush. Written in October 1919 it is addressed to 'My darling Div: D' and is signed 'All my love & a big kiss to you, From Your always fond & sentimental, Plain Jane'. The letter itself explains that, 'My time in the W.R.N.S. has been just one of the happiest times in my life, and its been just lovely having somebody one could just love, without being thought quite mad.'

As the war approached its conclusion, demobilisation loomed. With that came the question of what would follow. As early as April 1918 Helen wrote home to say that, 'Demobilisation, of a few people at any rate, seems to be coming nearer... One office for instance has completely shut up and the three Decoding Officers are on leave purely and simply because we don't know what is to happen to them – one is to be married next month so she is provided for but the other two are quite ready to go on at their job if they are wanted. I don't think it at all likely that H.Q. will want them however.'

One of her old VAD friends wrote from France just before the Armistice and confessed, 'I don't think I shall ever be able to settle down & do nothing at all, but the question is "what can one do?" I suppose something at home but I think it will be very difficult.'

The question of what might now be done was an important one. The war had dominated lives for over four years and even those not directly involved in the fighting would have devoted hours to the war effort, if only knitting socks, scarves or balaclavas, or making bandages, as at Quebec House in Kent amongst many other places.

Independent lives

As their husbands left for active service, women accepted responsibilities of many kinds, not just at home but also, for example, running small businesses such as cleaning windows and sweeping chimneys. One thing Cis Dawnay took over from her husband Guy was the sale of Beningbrough Hall. She was clearly a very resourceful woman and on 30 August 1916 she wrote to tell him that many of the rooms were 'bare of furniture ... quite cleared out! ... In a way I don't really mind as now one feels one has so entirely got back to the spirit of the house – We have got the shell of the house and very little else.'

The Dawnay property was eventually sold by auction in the autumn, the *Yorkshire Herald* reporting on Wednesday 15 November that over £100,000 was realised for various lots and that 'The actual sale only occupied the space of 13 minutes'.

Many women became aware that the war offered opportunities. It allowed them an unchaperoned, independent existence that would have

been unimaginable only a few years before. VAD nurse Margaret Van Straubenzee wrote in her memoir that it 'was my first taste of emancipation, being away from a sheltered home and standing on my own feet. I was completely unfitted to face the World, quite ignorant of all sex matters, very shy and unsophisticated.'

Her adventures appear enjoyable but relatively innocent. On one occasion she and three friends were in Guildford and 'got "picked up" by some Australian officers who were pretty well "oiled"! They … wanted to drive us up to town and take us to a show. I was against the plan … but two of the nurses went, and myself and the other were content to do a local flick with our two Aussies, and a grand time we had too.'

It seems not all the young women were quite so restrained. Describing an incident that took place at Christmas 1918, one of Helen Beale's WRNS colleagues told her 'the girls all went to a dance at the R.N.V.R. Wireless Club & had a glorious time with leave to be out till midnight! All my girls came in, but that naughty little Westcott stayed out all night! She turned up in the afternoon of Boxing Day & said she had been to a Dance at Hythe & had stayed with friends! Miss Wall wired her sister in London & she, the sister, says she is only sixteen!'

Above: Recovering soldiers with their nurse on the lawn at Morden Hall Park. Fresh air was considered healthy for patients.

Right: News of Rowland Winn's marriage was broken by the *Daily Mirror* in 1915. Later he wrote to his father from France, saying, 'I am quite sure you know that we would have given anything rather than that it should have been brought to your notice in the sudden + unpleasant way it was.'

It was hardly surprising that young men and women, away from parental supervision and in the stress of war, should have pushed boundaries in ways that would have been unthinkable only a few years earlier. In 1918, Sergeant Butcher at Stonehenge aerodrome was checking the rear fuselage of a Handley Page bomber which had just returned from a cross-country flight and was disgusted to find 'that the mechanics had two WRAF [Women's Royal Air Force] girls on board in overalls. In those days there were no checks on passengers: so this was how the war was drawing to a close, at least in England.' For him it showed 'just how much the spirit of the Service had deteriorated in four years.' Perhaps to others it might have seemed an enterprising lark.

He would have been even more appalled by the impropriety of Vita Sackville-West when that same year she dressed as a man and took a taxi to Hyde Park Corner. There she strolled around Mayfair smoking cigarettes and buying one from a boy who addressed her as 'Sir' and where she was also 'accosted now and then by women'. To her it was all immense fun, and 'the extraordinary thing was, how natural it all was'. In Bond Street she met up with her lover Violet Keppel and travelled to Orpington where they stayed in lodgings as husband and wife. In the morning they took the train to Knole where they sneaked into the stables, allowing Vita the chance to change back into her ordinary attire.

Scandal

Women had smoked cigarettes before 1914, some had gone to bed together and actresses had married the sons of important houses, but somehow the war seemed to accelerate behaviour once thought immoral or immodest. When the *Daily Mirror* revealed in April 1916 that Rowland Winn, heir to Nostell Priory, had married a chorus girl, it caused such a scandal that he was sacked from the Grenadier Guards for conduct unbecoming to an officer. It was deemed particularly disgraceful as the regiment's commander was His Majesty the King.

Rowland's parents Lord and Lady St Oswald were equally shocked, not least because they only heard of the marriage when they read about it in the newspaper. He was naturally very contrite and wrote to his father from France,

LORD ST. OSWALD'S HEIR MARRIES AN ACTRESS.

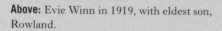

Above: Evie Winn in 1919, with eldest son, Rowland.

Above right: Lady Mabel St Oswald, 1910. The contrast in fashion with her daughter-in-law less than a decade later is notable.

Right: Eva White, munitionette. Her short hair and practical clothes, including trousers, marked her as a very modern woman.

'My dear Pa

Just a line to say how very pleased I was to hear from Mummy that you
had met my wife. As far as I could gather from Mummy's letter you were
favourably impressed, + liked her. At any rate she wrote + told me you
were extremely nice to her; + I only hope you really understand that she is
anything but the average "chorus girl".

By the summer of 1916 Rowland's new wife, Evie, was pregnant. With Rowland away at
war, Lord and Lady St Oswald agreed to pay the rent on the couple's London house. This
was taken by his son as an indication that his marriage had been accepted. He wrote
gratefully to his father saying, 'I don't know how to thank you enough for all you have
done for us, for the way in which you have taken to my Eve … it is such as relief when one
is out here, to know that she is being well looked after.' Despite its unpropitious start,
their marriage appears to have been a happy one.

War work

Evie Winn's newly privileged lifestyle was in distinct contrast to that of a neighbour at
Nostell Priory, Eva White. Eva was twenty-one when the war broke out and working at a
confectioners in Wakefield. But when the man she hoped to marry was killed in the
Dardanelles in 1915 she left her job and began working as a 'Barnbow Lass' at Barnbow
Munitions Factory near Leeds.

By 1916 the workforce at Barnbow numbered sixteen thousand on a 200-acre site. It
was described locally as a 'city within a city' and days at the factory were long and
arduous. Travelling by special bus with other workers, Eva worked eight hours a day, six
days a week, packing shells with explosives. It was perilous. This became only too
apparent in December that year when 'Room 42' blew up. The explosion killed thirty-five
women and injured many more. Yet despite the tragedy, Barnbow's workforce remained
resolute and returned to its vital role the next day.

By coincidence of name, when Eva married in May 1917 it was to another Rowland.
He was Rowland Stewart Hepworth, a miner and nephew of the groundskeeper at Nostell
Priory. She continued working at the factory until peace was declared, when she received a
certificate thanking her for the 'excellent services' she had rendered.

By the end of the war there were more than 1.6 million women working in factories,
the majority in munitions. 'Munitionettes', also known as 'Canary girls' because TNT is
toxic and repeated exposure turns the skin yellow, were distinctive in appearance. This
was not just because of their complexion, but because they wore trousers. Working in
grimy factories with greasy floors, dresses were simply impractical and could be dangerous
if snagged on machinery. It was a sign of increasing equality with men.

Wearing trousers was an outward sign of independence, but even those working in
more traditional clothes were still hugely emancipated compared to pre-war days. For one
thing, they were being paid higher wages than ever before. For another, hundreds of

thousands of women had taken over male jobs. They were welcomed almost everywhere with reluctance, but by 1918 female staff were working in banks and the Post Office, behind counters in shops and as clerks in offices. In Grantham, two women police officers were employed to dissuade local girls from drifting into prostitution, lured by the proximity of 20,000 men in the Machine Gun Corps at Belton House. Subject to some derision, the officers patrolled alleys, courtyards and passages where assignations might take place.

Women were also employed on the railways after 300,000 men had left to join the forces. At first they were taken on to do paperwork, but were finally hired as ticket collectors, train washers, porters, dining-car and signal-box attendants. Although paid half the rate of their male colleagues for the same work, it was still double what they might have earned in domestic service.

Helen Beale's brother, Sam, lost two of his maids to the railways. He told Helen, 'After 6 years Kate and Mary are both leaving on our return from Standen in the New Year – to go as train-conductors – which is the … ideal of every Glasgow maiden at the present moment, owing to the wages – 27/- a wk. & your uniform & spats, hat & cardigan jacket to boot.'

Above: *Voluntary Land Workers in a Flax Field*, Randlophe Schwabe, 1919. 18,000 tons of flax was needed every year to weave canvas to cover aeroplanes. The workers slept in ex-army bell tents (as seen in the background).

Right: Land Army girls were housed at Gibside Hall, Tyne and Wear (now derelict). Initially they were billeted in the servants' quarters, but finding their rooms too draughty and cold, they were eventually moved into the main body of the hall.

Servant crisis

The loss of servants was a huge preoccupation during the war years as men joined the army and women left for other jobs. Almost as an aside, Sam asked Helen in a letter of July 1916, 'Do you remember Fred Brown our footman? Wise tells me he is killed.' A few months earlier he had told her that his cook had left, though not to go into munitions but he thought because 'it was the introduction of margarine for cooking that started the fuss, & a general feeling that war economy was not for the likes of her, so she's going to marry our ineligible [as a soldier] chauffeur.'

As the war ended, many people hoped that women would return to their former duties as servants. Often, they were disappointed; Helen Beale's sister, Amy, had 'been in despair for maids' and wrote to ask her if there might be 'a kitchen maid for me amongst your staff'. Helen replied that regrettably, she couldn't 'fit her out with any really nice demobilized Wrens suitable for her household'.

Land girls

Although domestic service was regarded as a low class of employment it still represented better options than farm work. This posed huge problems during the war as more than 100,000 agricultural labourers had left for the army by early 1915. In nearby Burwash at the end of that year there were only six men not in the forces while one hundred and fifty had already joined up and Rudyard Kipling observed that 'all the conversation turns on

the six black sheep'. After conscription was introduced he had only one man 'over age to look after 160 acres of land and 27 cattle.'

The labour shortage was a deep crisis and it looked as though employing women was the only solution. A variety of organisations such as the Women's National Land Service Corps (WNLSC) and the Women's War Agricultural Committee were formed to recruit female workers. As a supposed incentive they were given armlets to wear after they had accomplished 30 days or 240 hours' work on the land. However, they were only paid 18s a week while under instruction and 20s once qualified. Kate, Mary and Eva would all have been earning far more than that on the trains or at Barnbow.

Signing herself 'A Woman Farmer', Beatrix Potter wrote from Hill Top about the shortage to *The Times* in March 1916. She said that the 'supply of women is undoubtedly affected by the competition of munition work. I pass no opinion as to whether munitions workers are extravagantly paid; I only know that farmers cannot compete with their wages. Three girls have gone from adjoining farms here; they expect to earn at least £2 wages per week. They are trained dairymaids and milkers, but totally inexperienced in mechanics.'

The dress women wore when working on the land attracted enormous hostility. When Lady Edith Vane-Tempest-Stewart of Mount Stewart wrote to *The Times* on the subject of women in agriculture, she received a huge volume of abuse from those who considered women wearing breeches to be perverted, immoral or obscene.

Lady Edith had formed the Women's Legion in 1915. Its function was to train women to work in roles previously undertaken by men and she worked particularly hard to promote the use of female labour in agriculture. They were to prove vital to the war effort. By July 1917 there were 1,000 women working full time on farms in the Surrey area and 944 part time workers, Lord Onslow of Clandon Park later conceding that they had proved 'not unsatisfactory.'

Above: Betty Colyer-Fergusson of Ightham Mote, right, in Land Army action.

Another reluctant host to female labourers was Rudyard Kipling who made Rye Green Farm House available as hostel accommodation for Land Army girls. Lanhydrock also took on the employment of eleven Cornish girls, who had applied to join the Women's Land Army at an assessment day held there. Lady Clifden was 'very anxious to have nice girls' of the industrial class and promised that 'they will be well looked after'.

The girls at Lanhydrock were employed on the estate woodland 'cross cutting and faggoting'. Across the country as a whole, about four hundred women worked as foresters, producing timber for use as trench supports and packing cases. Some undertook wood sawing in the deeply wooded Northumberland hillsides at Rothbury for Lord Armstrong of Cragside.

Digging deep

Prior to the war, the country had been highly dependent on food supplies from overseas, in 1913 importing 78.7 per cent of its wheat. The German U-boat campaign that sank so much shipping threatened the country with starvation so over the course of the war an extra 2.5 million acres of land was taken into cultivation, including the park at Lanhydrock, which was used for growing cereals. In places such as Waddesdon Manor and Cliveden, flowerbeds were given over to growing vegetables and even the

Left: *The Women's Land Army and German Prisoners*, Randlophe Schwabe, 1918. Women of the Land Army, wearing WLA armbands, gather in the harvest with prisoners of war. The women were supposed to work separately from the Germans. Clearly this did not always happen.

Queen was pictured in her garden lifting potatoes. The policy worked and by 1918 the country was producing 8,574,000 tons of grain and 9,223,000 tons of potatoes, as compared to 6,086,000 tons and 7,605,000 tons respectively in 1914.

In addition to the thousands of women working full time in farming, harvests required extra labour and that in 1918 called upon 15,000 schoolboys and Boy Scouts along with 30,000 POWs. Prisoners of war helped out on a regular basis in many places and between August and December 1918, Lord Rothschild paid the POW camp local to Waddesdon Manor £110. 13s. 6d for their hire.

University students also contributed to harvesting for short periods while children in many country areas were released early from school to take up full-time posts. In 1916, the parents of Charles Neville, a pupil at West Clandon School, near Clandon Park, in Surrey, applied for him to begin work at the age of thirteen on a local farm for a minimum wage of 7/- a week. And in the autumn of 1917, arrangements were made at West Clandon for its pupils, as in schools across the country, to collect horse chestnuts – the chestnuts being a source of acetone used in the manufacture of munitions.

Life on the land

If some farmers regarded female workers as 'worse pests than weeds', that was emphatically not the case with Cis Dawnay. In her last summer at Beningbrough while arranging its auction, she became very involved with the various farms. Her letters to her soldier husband Guy reflect her delight in the work and confidence in the women.

Writing in May 1916, she told him of a great ally she had made in Mrs Routledge who 'called last night! … I thought her a very active strong minded lady! She is engaged in making a local Register of Female Land Workers! I was very glad to see her as she cd tell me of all the village people willing to work.'

A few months later she reports, 'I have had discussions with my ladies on the farm about their wages – I hear the farmers round say £1 a week is too much, & the farm hands say that we pay them at a higher rate than they are payed – so I went to the ladies and explained my difficulties with the result that they now are working 8½ hours a day for 18/- We arranged it quite amicably between us – They are a great success, and come up to tea here on Sundays – The children take them strawberries.'

Things got even better a few weeks later when another advance was made for equality with men. She declared, 'Triumph! Miss Proctor is now undertaking to drive the milk float into York! She went this morning with the man – tomorrow she goes by herself – Do you think it risky?'

Although not born to farming, she understood the essentials and put forward strong views, 'Now about the farm. We are making 2 Big mistakes. We are farming on too big a scale to do well. We are very undermanned – the result being there are grumbles, the work inefficiently done – and all scientific and good farming is neglected… The presence of the ladies has undoubtedly raised the standard, but there is lots that should & cd be done.'

Losing a loved one

Cis was clearly a remarkably strong and determined woman, as were others such as Lady Clandon, Helen Beale and Teresa Hulton (better known as Lady Berwick). Not all enjoyed their advantages of privilege or personality. One such was the widow of Lance Corporal P.C. Newman. In April 1916, she wrote to Lt Colonel Leonard Messel at Nymans asking for his help following the death of her husband, Lance-Corporal P.C. Newman.

Leonard was of part-German parentage and so not allowed on active service, but he remained busy in Sussex preparing troops for front-line duty. He also had a vast number of correspondents whose letters create a composite picture of the war in its many varied aspects. Daisy Newman's expressed the belief that 'when the hardest of the bitterest is over, I shall feel proud that my husband died in the most glorious cause, like a good sportsman playing the straight game to the last.'

His death, though, left her struggling to cope and she went on to explain, 'the only thing I am really in difficulties over, is how to obtain what was due to my Husband, such as his back pay and £15 Bounty for extended services, also I would like to have a copy of his "will" as ... the Insurance Company refuse to pay me any money until I can produce this... My health has broken down due to the worry.'

Daisy Newman's letter shows the practical problems faced by the bereaved, especially those not well off.

Below: Alda, Lady Hoare. Painted by St George Hare, 1910.

Diary of despair

One woman to articulate her grief in vivid, painful terms was Alda, Lady Hoare of Stourhead on the death of her only child, Harry. He had been gravely injured at Mughar Ridge in Palestine on 13 November 1917. Despite the severity of his wounds, his parents had been sent news at the beginning of December that he was 'out of danger doing well'. A further report from the War Office then arrived to tell them he was 'Dangerously ill 9th'. Alda's diary records the following few days in which the news gives alternate reason for hope and despair,

Thursday December 13

Harry is never out of our thoughts & we talk & talk of him. But I keep 'going'.

Friday December 14

I not out. Ever awaiting, longing & dreading news Harry… I do not leave house; wait ever telegram of Harry. But at 3 I walked twice the length South Lawn for air…

Sunday December 16

Very cold grey dreary day. Snowing hard till 12. Henry advised me not go Church… We'd earnestly hoped by 10 a.m. to have had wire from Harry's Doctor, which should have been here at, & any time after 7 p.m. on Sunday. But none has come. We read the Service together in 'South-Room' & together prayed for him.

Thursday December 20

Fine. Snow all around. Still no telegrams. I got out on 'South Lawn Walk' 2.45 to 3. Shall we never hear? In his letter of Nov 23rd he said 'he'd sent us a wire', that we never got.

Friday December 21

At 9.50, in 'South-Room', at last come 2 wires, both dated Dec 18th, one from our own son's Doctor saying 'Wired you fifteenth condition improved – since, still improving'. The 2nd wire is from Freddy Wingfield-Digby: 'Saw Harry yesterday – Progressing satisfactorily'. Together we knelt & humbly thanked God for his unspeakable mercy… In afternoon I gave away at school my prizes to all my children. Henry went into Mere re our Xmas gifts to Mere Hospital… Snow thick lies all round. Very cold.

Saturday December 22

In 'South-Room' I wrote my Xmas-letters – told to all the good news of Harry. At 2 p.m. in the 'South-Room' they bring me another wire, from his Doctor 'Alexandria, Wed.y 19th, 1.30 p.m. Serious relapse. Very dangerous'. I wire back imploring earliest news… I pray up in his bedroom, by his bedside… Henry returned at 7.15 p.m. – I told him. We are prepared for the worst. God give us strength to hear it.

Sunday December 23

A sad sad day. We went to morning-church… I wept today hidden by our old pew. We spent rest of day together in South-Room as sun sank in a red glory. 'Oh Henry perhaps it means better news' I dared to hope a moment. He shook his head.

Monday Xmas-Eve

At 11.55 in 'South Room' where both had put in a hard morning's business, to keep from the awful dread, came, just as we finished, the realisation. 'He died of wounds on 20th December'.

Tuesday Xmas-Day

Henry & I spent all today in the 'South-Room'… We have read the Xmas Service to ourselves & sat at our lonely Xmas dinner, with his empty chair.

Sir Henry and Alda later learned that Harry had in fact died on December 19. They never recovered from his loss.

Shopping spree

Alda Hoare and Lady St Oswald had much in common but much that set them apart. For while both came from aristocratic families, lived in beautiful houses and were imposing figures, Alda seems to have had a strong sense of duty, while Lady St Oswald was less driven. Ben Mitchell, a patient at the Mere Hospital, was obviously very impressed by Lady Hoare. He said, 'she was a lady in more respects than one. She was charming and made a point of visiting each bed in the hospital and did not seem to mind how long she spent chatting to the men.'

Lady St Oswald, Mabel Winn, by contrast, tended to spend more time with her family and on her social life. Most of her time was spent in London rather than at Nostell Priory with her invalid husband, and seems to have been filled by gossips with friends, parties, balls and other such functions.

She also liked spending money and in one shop alone in January 1919 spent £25.19s.9d on three camisoles, one tight dress, one pair of knickers, one chemise and a blouse.

This would have been a huge sum of money to women such as Eva White earning £2 per week in a munitions factory or a farm girl working for even less. Mabel also spent lavishly on such things as flowers, perfume, gloves and hairdressing. She died in the Spanish flu epidemic of 1918–19, which took a greater number of lives even than the war. Her husband's death followed less than a month later. The old order was passing in more ways than one.

Votes for women

As the war drew to a close, politicians began to plan for a General Election. There was a problem, however, since under existing electoral rules men had to be resident in the UK for twelve months prior to an election to be eligible to vote. Yet many had been away for years. A change of the rules was required, which gave women's rights campaigners the opportunity to claim that women had been fulfilling men's jobs, had often been near the front line and had been exposed to equal danger through bombing raids. They argued that if the electoral system was to be changed to allow men who had been serving overseas to vote, it should be amended to give women the vote as well.

For once there was little disagreement. The Representation of the People Bill was passed in March 1917 and became law eleven months later. Women were granted suffrage – but it was limited to those over the age of thirty who were married or those over thirty-five if graduates. Ironically, this excluded people like Eva White who had contributed significantly. She had worked at Barnbow for more than three years under several Ministers of Munitions including David Lloyd George and Winston Churchill but at twenty-six she was still too young to vote.

Left: Nancy, Lady Astor, being presented to Parliament between Lord Balfour (left) and David Lloyd George, 1919.

The first woman actually to win a seat in Parliament was the Irish radical Countess Markievicz. She had been imprisoned many times for her political activities, including a leading role in the Easter Uprising in Dublin in 1916 – and despising Westminster she declined to take her place there. Lady Nancy Astor of Cliveden thus became the first woman to sit in the House of Commons when she won a Plymouth by-election in 1919.

She entered the chamber flanked by David Lloyd George and Arthur Balfour, one the current Prime Minister, the other a former PM. For women, it was a victory of sorts.

3. A WAR OF MOVEMENT, 1914

On a sultry July evening in 1914 Henry Page Croft MP, later Lord Croft of Croft Castle, was in conversation with an 'exceedingly beautiful American girl'. She asked how he proposed to spend his holidays and was derisive when informed he was off to join his territorial battalion in camp. She told him, 'I cannot understand how any English gentleman can so waste his time, our men are busy in the States doing things that matter.'

Croft was furious, but explained that 'every country gentleman, except a few of Quaker blood held commissions in the Territorial Army, if not already in the regular forces', and that 'while inconvenient', many felt it was their patriotic duty.

Frederick Hughes, a miner born in a cottage on the Chirk Castle estate came from a very different background to Henry. Yet he too was a Territorial, having joined below age at fifteen in 1913 and was full of enthusiasm. According to a memoir his brother Edward wrote in 1920, Fred was 'a regular attendant at all the appointed drills' and when working nights and unable to attend an evening session, 'would go down to the Drill Hall in the morning and practice'.

He was excited about going to the training camp in Aberystwyth, was there when war broke out and immediately mobilised. All other Territorials were too, though many people doubted their worth. Edward recalled, 'they were taunted and ridiculed, and in the estimation of those who pretended to know them they were considered as useless for the battlefield.' In fact, they were to prove invaluable.

Henry Croft's regiment left for France on 4 November, 1914. In his autobiography, *My Life of Strife*, he records, 'we marched through the town in the early hours of the morning and arrived at the station just as day dawned. The sun rose, a band played, and we entrained for the great adventure.' Fred sailed from Southampton the following day. He was sixteen years old.

The Territorials were essential since in the years before the war cutbacks and restructuring had seen the regular army reduced to less than 250,000, around half of which were garrisoned abroad in different parts of the Empire. With Reservists and Territorials, the theoretical strength of the army was approximately 700,000 although when war broke out, regular army troops stationed in Britain numbered 125,000. Machine guns and heavy artillery were lacking and the Royal Flying Corps consisted of 84 planes. This was opposed to a conscript German army of 5.4 million men.

German strategy from the outset had involved smashing through Belgium to attack France on her undefended flank. It was defence of neutral Belgium that had drawn Britain into the war and it was on its southern border with France that British troops first met the weight of German advance. Heavily outnumbered and outgunned, the British dug in at Mons in an effort to gain time for the French to regroup.

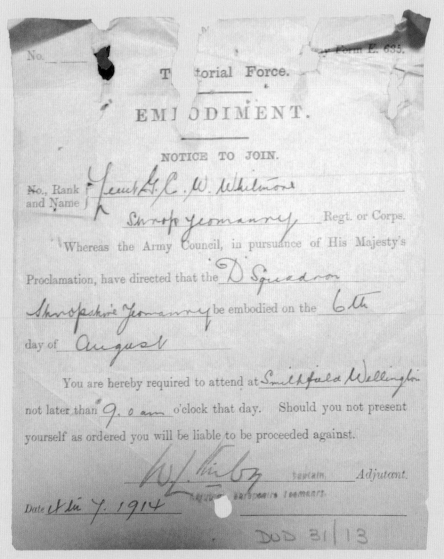

Left: Call-up papers of Geoffrey Wolryche Whitmore of Dudmaston Hall, Shropshire. He was a member of the Shropshire Yeomanry, his call up arriving only days after the outbreak of war.

Retreat

The battle began on 23 August, but the line couldn't be held and the following day it was decided to retreat to a more defensible position in France. Fighting was intense, since although numerically much smaller, the British Army was a volunteer force comprised of long-serving men who were all highly trained marksmen. Robert Vereker of Overbeck's had joined the Grenadier Guards in September 1913. Aged just twenty-one, he was shot and killed while trying to draw a wounded corporal out of the range of fire. In an account of the action in the *The Kingsbridge Gazette*, a captured German is reported to have said of British resistance during the retreat: 'We had never expected anything like it; it was staggering.'

Stephen Cawley of Berrington Hall was killed a few days later, on 1 September. He had joined the Hussars in 1898 and served in many parts of the Empire. His death was described by a fellow officer,

Below: Stephen Cawley of Berrington Hall, Herefordshire, in the dress uniform of the Hussars.

'*Our Brigade was attacked soon after dawn by a force double our number – a Cavalry Division with twelve guns. Owing to a thick mist they managed to get within 600 yards of us; 350 horses of the Bays stampeded, and their men went after them, and the 'L' Battery, R.H.A., was cut to pieces. The occasion was one which called for personal example and Major Cawley ... went to help to restore order and get the broken remnants into their places. The situation being met, and everyone being in his place, he joined the advanced line, and was almost immediately killed by a piece of shell. The splendid manner in which he met his death in deliberately facing the awful fire in order to help ... is only what his whole life has told us to expect.*'

Confusion

Jim Pennyman of Ormesby Hall served with the Kings Own Scottish Borderers (KOSB) and kept a diary of the war's first days. According to this, they arrived in France on 15 August in heavy rain and 'spent an uncomfortable night in the docks in a shed'. The KOSB were involved in the battle at Mons on 23 August and he described 'our first experience of killing people: it was rather horrible, but satisfactory.'

The account he gives of the next few weeks seems typical of the early days of the war, a curious mixture of horror, confusion, movement and holiday. Disorganisation was perhaps inevitable, however orderly the retreat. At one stage a group of men was seen that they 'thought were enemy and fired. Then they waved their Glengarries and we saw they were Borderers.' Later they in turn were shot at by British forces, Jim noting, 'I was never able to find out who fired on us, but it wasn't the Germans.'

Once the British had fallen back to their intended defensive line on 24 August, it was found impossible to hold and the retreat continued for the next two weeks, involving a series of battles. One of these was on 26 August at Le Cateau where Jim and his men took over some trenches which 'were well dug and well sighted, but only very short, holding a platoon at most, and very far apart'.

About dawn orders were received to hold the trenches and 'not to retire under any circumstances'. He records, 'About 7 a.m. we saw enormous

Below: Hand-drawn plan of troop dispositions at Battle of Le Cateau (otherwise known as the Battle for Ligny), August 1914 by Major Archie Montgomery of Gunby Hall, Lincolnshire.

masses of Germans deploying about 3 miles ahead and realised we were
in for a big thing.' He was right. It is said that 55,000 British troops
faced 140,000 of the enemy and that at no other stage of the war were
the odds so devastatingly unbalanced. 'Soon their shells began to come
and battery after battery opened upon us – searching the whole place…
Our artillery replied, but it was obvious that they were hopelessly
outnumbered.' Somehow the order to hold fast had not reached the
forward platoons who withdrew from their trenches, giving Jim no
alternative but to leave as well.

By the end of the following day he calculated 'we had done 35 miles since Le Cateau and the men were beat to such a degree that it was more like herding sheep than leading soldiers.' Eventually on Friday 28 August he joined up with others from the regiment near Pontoise and together they were 'quite an imposing party'. It had been a tough introduction to war. During the week they had 'marched over one hundred miles, fought three battles and two scraps'.

Things remained unclear and over the next few days Jim constantly found uncertainty about where he was or what he should be doing. On Friday 4 September he wrote, 'About this time we were very puzzled as to what the general situation was…' on Wednesday 9, 'I galloped up and the section followed, but I had difficulty in finding out my exact task… I had not so much as a glimmering on the situation…' and on Sunday 13,

Left: Jim Pennyman as a captain in 1917.

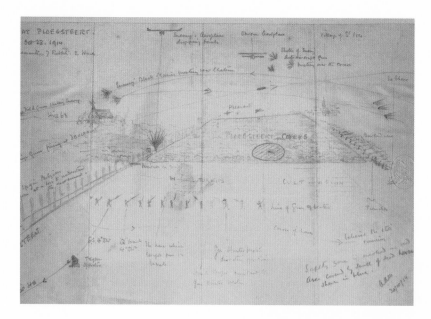

'During one of the halts I felt I was going to sleep and told off a man to keep touch with the rear of the Battalion. When I woke up I found we had lost touch.'

Jim wrote relatively little about the battles in which he fought, but he obviously saw much of the ugly side of war. On Thursday 10 he 'marched all day through unsavoury German remains. There was debris of all kinds along the road, consisting of waggons and things they had got rid of in order to hasten their progress, a dead horse every ten yards and a fair number of soldiers.'

Tip top

Despite the weariness, disorder and horror, Jim's account of the war's early days has a lightness; almost a suggestion of holiday adventure. In part this had to do with the fact that it was still summer with the exciting freshness of events, the countryside largely unspoiled. On the first day of the retreat he commented, 'Fortunately it was harvest time and we could generally get straw. Anyone who has three sheaves of straw for his bed has no cause for complaint. I found a farm and got some eggs for the mess.'

A couple of days later while marching he 'noticed some horrible looking carcases in the mud by the road side.' Although 'dirty and beastly' he discovered on closer examination that they were 'perfectly good British ration meat'. Shortly after, they passed a kitchen garden and helped themselves to potatoes and sweet vegetables and later met 'an old lady, who had a cauldron. Into this we put all our treasures and filled up with water... The stew was absolutely tip top.' As he describes it, the episode sounds more like a Scout-camp ramble than an incident in full-scale war.

Another reason for Jim's sometimes jaunty tone was the welcoming friendliness of the French and Belgian peasants. Later many were to become cynical and exploitative, but at this early stage the British troops were seen as heroic fighters against German tyranny. Almost everywhere they were met with hospitality. At one place where they stayed on 1 September they filled up their flasks with brandy at the farmer's request, 'knowing that the Germans would only take it next day.'

A day or two previously they had stayed in an abandoned farm which the enemy had occupied. Anxious not to be blamed for the untidiness, Jim says, 'We left a note for the owners of the house when they should come back, thanking them for shelter and saying that it was the Germans, and not us who had made such a mess of their house.' Such innocent good manners would have seemed laughable by 1918.

Knocked down

The sense that the war in this initial stage was a sort of game is hinted at by the simile Jim used when describing the injury he sustained on Monday 14 September. He said it was a sensation 'like a blow with a cricket ball in the chest'. It was much more serious and 'knocked me clean down, and I remember shouting as I fell and bleeding profusely at the mouth. I felt quite certain that I was a "gonner".'

Wounded about 2 p.m., Jim lay untreated until 7 p.m. He was comatose most of the following day but when conscious was told there was 'great difficulty in getting stretcher cases away, as the bridge behind us was blown up and the enemy were close'. Overnight he and others were transported in an ambulance wagon and by 'springless motor lorries' to the railhead at Oulchy.

From there, on Thursday 17 he was put into a rail truck fitted with 'spring hooks to hold the stretchers. There were about six of us in the carriage and an R.A.M.C. [Royal Army Medical Corps] orderly. I had been cute (or selfish) enough to annex a second blanket to put underneath me; even with this addition a stretcher is a very cold and hard thing to lie on for the best part of a week.' Eventually, after forty-eight hours in the train and a trip in a motor ambulance, Jim arrived at No. 8 Field Hospital, Rouen. He had 'had no food but a little beef tea and practically no sleep for five days and nights' and 'felt very done up'. He was in pain and when he did sleep had nightmares about the Germans in which 'I was always trying to get away from somewhere, but could never do so, because I could not find my men'. At last, on 29 September he arrived in hospital in London. For the time being he was safe.

Antwerp and Ypres

Below: Winston Churchill, First Lord of the Admiralty, (left) and Jack Seely, Secretary of State for War, at the Guards Review in Hyde Park in 1913. Jack was on active service throughout the war. Aged only twenty, his eldest son, Frank, was killed in the Battle of Arras in 1917.

Across the Channel the situation worsened. At the beginning of October it looked as though Antwerp was about to be taken by the Germans. Plans were made to withdraw Belgian troops to Ostend, but on 3 October the British Government persuaded the Belgians to delay evacuation, promising to send reinforcements. Winston Churchill was sent to liaise with the Belgian Government and report back on the situation.

Once on the scene, Churchill took charge with typical energy. His old friend Colonel Jack Seely, later of Mottistone Manor on the Isle of Wight, reached there shortly afterwards and recorded in his memoirs, 'From the moment I arrived it was apparent that the whole business was in Winston's hands. He dominated the whole place… So great was his influence that I am convinced that with 20,000 British troops he could have held Antwerp against any onslaught.'

In the event, British reinforcements never arrived. Winston was recalled to London and Belgian forces evacuated the city, leaving 1,400 men of the Royal Naval Division to be interned in Holland. It was seen as a humiliating defeat and damaged Churchill's reputation, yet the defence of Antwerp delayed the German advance and allowed the Allies to reach Ypres before them. Strategically vital, possession of Ypres meant control of the ports through which the British army was supplied. Had Antwerp fallen earlier, this might have been lost.

By mid-October, the 1st Battle of Ypres had begun. It was crucial to hold the town and fighting was intense. Alan Dawnay wrote to his brother Guy of Beningbrough Hall about his position in a thick wood at Zillebeke on 7 November, 'Of course we have made our section <u>very</u> strong indeed … but it is not a peaceful place to be in, as apart from their snipers … they throw their rotten bombs into our trenches all night long, & occasional heavy shells as well, & their extreme closeness means keeping up a continual state of readiness against a rush.

'One more word about this wood generally – it is really the most gruesome place! When we arrived it was thick with German corpses (800 were I believe buried in one clearing) & since then we go on finding most unpleasant things … for instance, 2 Germans hanging from a tree, & 3 others tied to trees & shot, presumably by their own people – then we picked up a wretched man from the Worcesters who had lain out wounded for 7 days & was still alive, & another who cd stick it no longer & had cut his throat with a bayonet!'

Henry Page Croft arrived in the wood at Zillebeke with the Hertforshire Regiment a few days later. He described the village in *Twenty-Two Months Under Fire*, 'A battered church still looked like a church, houses dishevelled and war-broken still stood tottering or with roof stripped bare; but ruin, stark ruin, seemed to stare at us from every side.' From there, he entered the wood, 'The moon was now out and a hard frost had set in as we wended our way through the pine trees.'

Holding the line

Henry had arrived at Ypres on 11 November. It was already war damaged, 'The rain ceased, and we entered the ancient city under a bright moon. The stricken town was very silent, although in the distance we could hear the incessant artillery duel. Sometimes we had to go slow, owing to the ruins of a house being scattered over the road; here we saw houses still burning after the day's bombardment, then a body huddled in a corner, and we knew that this was war.'

Even among the ruins there were elements of humour, as he found when he arrived at brigade headquarters, 'my impressions of which were a little cottage with several holes in the wall, considerable noise from artillery all round, liquid freezing mud everywhere; and in this scene of noisy desolation two privates … splashing through the mire after an old hen … we had to wait about in the bitter cold, but on being welcomed into the guard room by the sergeant of the guard we were presented with cups of steaming chicken broth, and I found my sympathies, which had previously been with the hen, were now wholly on the side of the guard.'

The Western Front was still a new experience for him – and a new form of warfare. He was told it was 'advisable to keep the men in the holes provided for them (dugouts were a later invention, and no one had up to now had time to dig trenches to any depth).' The war of movement was coming to an end, and defensive positions dug that were to remain virtually unchanged for almost four years.

The toll had been immense. More officers had been killed in the first hundred days of the war than in the previous hundred years. On entering a dugout not long after his arrival in France, Henry could only guess what the men he met had been through, 'Under the dim light of one candle some eight officers were gathered round a table, and it is hard to imagine signs of greater physical fatigue than were evidenced on their faces; but they were all typical officers of the old regular army: that type which never shows surprise and which considers every question with dignity and without emotion … and finding ourselves amongst these men with the distant look in their eyes which comes from continual strain, we felt we had entered a new world.'

Much later, in his 1948 autobiography *My Life of Strife*, he paid tribute to the men of the regular army who 'had been fighting almost incessantly through the retreat from Mons, the battles of the Aisne and the Marne, and then Ypres, were outnumbered by ten to one in bayonets, shelled all the time with no heavy guns to reply, and the German in command of the air.' Yet the line was held. Henry was at the Front that first Christmas and said it 'was celebrated at dawn with rapid fire… It was a cold, sharp day, and we received various gifts which friends at home had sent to us, and many a charcoal fire was busy cooking wonderful dishes along the trench. That night both sides sang carols and the firing ended.'

On the march

A few months later, William Armstrong of Cragside arrived in France with the Northumberland Fusiliers. It was 21 April 1915 and his first impressions would have been familiar to many. In his memoir, *My First Week in Flanders*, he wrote, 'It was a beautiful night, which made the march through the empty streets of the French port rather impressive. There was a silent hush over the whole place, except for the tramp, tramp of hob-nailed boots over the cobbled streets.'

Although it was already a very different war to that fought in August 1914, his account is in many ways similar to that by Jim Pennyman. After a train journey to Belgium, William reports, 'We spent a delightful day of rest amid charming scenery in the enjoyment of a really lovely day of early summer; it was hard to realise what we were doing there at all. We would forget, only to be brought back to earth by the rumbling of the guns, none too far away, and by the sight of a German aeroplane.'

From there, he headed to Ypres. It is said that a quarter of all British casualties in the entire war were sustained in that area. Like Henry Page

Right: William Watson Armstrong of Cragside. Ironically, Cragside's founder had made his fortune selling armaments. Industrialist and arms manufacturer, William George, 1st Baron Armstrong, sold weapons to both sides during the American Civil War and built ships for various nations including Japan and Russia.

THE
NORTHUMBERLAND
FUSILLIERS.

Croft, William arrived at night. 'The roar of the guns was tremendous. We marched past the famous Cloth Hall (even then badly knocked about), and began to move at the double, so as to escape being shelled… The cathedral was on fire, and made a glorious, but sad, spectacle. At this time it was still more or less intact, as were the majority of the deserted houses.'

Baptism of fire

It was not long before William Armstrong saw serious action and losses occurred. 'One shell, which burst a yard or two off me, killed two of my men and injured another. The two men displayed great heroism in their dying agony. One of them, Bob Young, as he was carried away, minus his legs, called upon an officer, who was almost overcome by the sight, to be a man… The battalion in these operations lost about 150 killed and wounded, including the two young Wakes (Wilf and Tom) of Bamburgh, both killed by the same shell.'

Shortly afterwards he was hit twice in the back by shrapnel. Like Jim Pennyman, he thought he was done for – 'any moment I expected would be my last… My position was a perilous one, as the Germans swept the plain with their murderous fire, and to stand up was certain death.' Helped by a comrade, he was able to struggle to shelter, 'Every movement was agonising, but at last we managed to reach the ditch and lie there exhausted… Soon others began to crawl into the ditch, including two very nice officers of the 6th N.F., who were most sympathetic.' Only later was he told that the sergeant who had pushed him into the ditch at the end of his painful trek had been 'blown to pieces immediately after by a shell'.

As the battle continued and it looked as though their position was going to be overrun by the enemy, William was helped by two others to a ruined farm. From there he was taken by stretcher to a safe zone and laid at the roadside.

Eventually William was moved by ambulance to Poperinghe and from there to Hazebrouck where he spent a month. 'The staff were terribly overworked, as the wounded and gassed cases were pouring in from the great battle, which was still raging… After about a month, I was able to be moved to No. 7 Stationary Hospital at Boulogne.' There his father arrived with a gramophone and William was much revived listening to 'Girls, Girls Everywhere' and 'Let's all Go Down the Strand'. At last on 25 June he was shipped back to England and taken to Lady Ridley's Hospital at 10 Carlton House Terrace in London and spent another 'two months being well nursed and surrounded by luxuries'. He finally reached Cragside on 28 September and received £250 as compensation for his wounds.

Both William Armstrong and Jim Pennyman recovered from their injuries and returned to the Western Front. Neither wrote accounts of their later experiences.

Left: William Watson Armstrong standing outside the main entrance, Cragside, Northumberland.

4. GALLIPOLI, 1915

The war that was to have been won by Christmas dragged on into 1915. With armies dug into trenches all the way from Belgium to Switzerland, ways were sought to seize initiative. In November 1914 Winston Churchill, as First Lord of the Admiralty, proposed a naval attack on the Dardanelles. If the Straits could be forced and battleships captured Constantinople (now Istanbul), Turkey might be knocked out of the war.

Like many of Churchill's plans, the concept was innovative and brilliant. Confidence was high. In a letter written on board ship to his mother on 20 July 1915, Sir Herbert Archer Croft of the Herefordshire Regiment wrote, 'I fancy this job won't be long and we shall be coming home unless kept for duty overseas for a time.' Ten days later, his excitement was still evident, when he wrote, 'The Rumours as to our movements are rampant… We left the quay last night and are now lying in the stream waiting for orders. Troopship after troopship comes in and there must be thousands of troops going and coming… We have no idea what our future movements will be. I shall not be at all surprised if this Dardanelles show is over very soon.'

The troopships observed by Sir Archer had in fact been assembling in the Mediterranean for months, following an initial attempt to take the Dardanelles Straits by battleship in March. This failure led to a decision to send an expeditionary force to the Gallipoli peninsula, led by Sir Ian Hamilton. He and his general staff, including Guy Dawnay of Beningbrough Hall, had no reliable maps of the area or information about Turkish forces and the slow build-up of troops in Egypt gave the Turks plenty of warning of an attack – and plenty of time to prepare their defences.

Had Churchill's initial plan of November 1914 been followed speedily and with resolve it might possibly have worked, changing the course of the war. When Allied troops finally went ashore on the peninsula in April 1915, they faced an almost impossible task. Many were from Australia and New Zealand, diverted to Gallipoli en route for the Western Front. Casualty rates were appalling. For every 100 yards gained, a thousand lives were lost. The attack on Beach V, (Cape Helles) on 25 April, was described by Guy Dawnay in a letter to his wife,

'The tows going in were met by a terrific fire from rifles, machine guns and pom-poms, and though a landing was actually effected that is all that can be said. The enemy's fire was all at close range, and the men who got ashore were unable even to get off the beach…

'The machine guns and pom-poms were so dug in as to be practically impossible to get at by fire… In addition to all this there was a wide, strong barbed wire entanglement right along the beach – almost impossible to get through – with several equally strong lines zigzagged across the amphitheatre higher up. I believe that every man who set foot on the beach must have been killed but for the fact that the beach itself was very narrow and that it was backed by a small low bank or little escarpment, all along which there was just room for men to shelter.'

Above: Sir Herbert Archer Croft (known as Archer), with son James. His family had lived at Croft Castle since 1086 but sold it in 1746. It was re-acquired by the Crofts in 1923 as home for James. After he was killed in World War II it passed to his relative, Henry Page Croft.

Left: Guy Dawnay. In *Seven Pillars of Wisdom*, TE Lawrence wrote of him, 'During the war he had the grief of planning the attack at Suvla (spoiled by incompetent tacticians).'

Suvla Bay

Not all the men who died on the peninsula were killed in action. Many succumbed to disease, including George Vernon of Sudbury Hall who died of dysentery. Conditions were terrible. Heat was intense, flies buzzed relentlessly and the stink of death was everywhere. It was into this that Sir Herbert Archer sailed for the attack on Suvla Bay at the beginning of August.

The landing at Suvla Bay had been relatively straightforward, but typical of the campaign as a whole, the advantage was not pressed. Had the Allied troops pushed on they might have gained the higher ground. As it was, they began to dig in on the lower slopes to consolidate their position. From then on, momentum was lost.

One description of the early stage of the battle comes in a letter from Sydney Beale of Standen to his sister, Helen, who was nursing in France. He wrote:

'It was an exceedingly muddled show, I'm afraid… Our own people got up to and in front of the line when the rest of the attack had come to a standstill; they were done and couldn't shove on again when we went on, so that a lot of ours got badly knocked about, and what was left of them came back to a continuation of their line. The scrapping went on all night, and next day, Aug 10th, the balance of the Division attacked through our line, but the Turks had spent the night digging and getting machine guns up, and though some them claimed to have been on the top of the hill they were told to take, none of them stopped any nearer than our line.'

Sydney's account was written on 9 September. Much later, in a letter of 29 November, Helen's sister Maggie passed on news of him received from 'one of the men invalided home' who told her 'how Syd came on three men asleep in a trench, just as three Turks had crept up and turned their machine gun at us. Syd and another officer shot the three Turks dead with their revolvers.'

These letters were received long after the actions they describe. When the landing took place families were desperate for information. Any news was quickly circulated. On 22 August, Sydney's mother, Margaret, wrote to Helen,

'I don't know whether you will have heard somehow that the 1/4 Sussex have been fighting & that C Campbell is wounded slightly and G Ridley also, we do not know how much, also 3 other officers, we think it must have been in that new landing at Suvla Bay & we dread the list of casualties amongst the men as it seems as though it is likely to be heavy.'

For King and Country

Above: The Welsh Casualty Clearing Station on 'A' beach, Suvla Bay. From *The Dardanelles* (1915), written and illustrated by Norman Wilkinson, official war artist.

On that casualty list were to appear the names of Duncan and Gwion Llewelyn Bowen Lloyd of Llanerchaeron. The brothers were killed seven days apart on 7 and 14 August. Also listed was Sir Herbert Archer Croft, 10th Baronet. His body was never found. Written on 14/15 September, an account of his death reached his mother in a letter from J.M. Leigh,

'You will probably have already heard from Capt. Capel and others the account of his tragic end – how he was leading them on and in his zeal and enthusiasm was separated from them and shot down by snipers who were firing in every direction – I cannot tell you how grieved I was to hear from them the account of his sad death … the only consolation one can offer is that he died fighting for his King and Country in a noble cause.

These sentiments were echoed by Sir Archer's brother, William, who at the time was serving in France. Ten days after J.M. Leigh's letter, he wrote,

'Darling Mother,
Esme has told me the news about dear old Archer.
I know how you feel about it and I cannot tell you how I feel for you…
Our grief is bitter at his loss but long after we have gone over our sons'
sons shall say "Sir Archer Croft died for his country in the Dardanelles"
and this will encourage our descendants to take a just pride in themselves
as Englishmen and try to emulate him.'

William's letter ends bleakly, 'It is raining hard today and not very encouraging as we go into the trenches tonight.' The Gallipoli campaign had never been fully thought through. Intended to be short in duration and designed to relieve pressure on the Western Front, the longer it dragged on the more troops and ammunition it required. There was never enough of either. The government in London briefly considered abandoning the campaign, decided against it but could not offer sufficient supplies. By September 1915, things were going from bad to worse.

Staff officers

One staff officer very much aware of this was Harold Cawley MP, of Berrington Hall. Harold had been a territorial officer with the 6th Manchesters before the war, and immediately joined his regiment on its outbreak. Although on landing at Gallipoli he had two horses hit before lunch, life at Divisional Headquarters was relatively without danger.

Eventually he could stand this no longer. Writing to one of his brothers he explained,

'Every combatant Officer who left Egypt with the Battalion has now been
killed or wounded, and more killed than wounded. In addition about
twelve new Officers have been hit, again mostly killed. As a consequence I
am going back to them. I have always felt rather a brute skulking behind
in comparative safety while my friends are being killed.'

Once back with the battalion, he rapidly proved his worth. His Adjutant wrote, 'We were completely without Company Officers of any seniority, and he adapted himself so quickly to the condition of life in the trenches, and was so sound in his judgments, that it was the greatest relief to us to have him.'

His Colonel was equally approving. 'When we went up to the front line I put him in charge of the firing trench, and it was due in a great measure to his coolness and bravery,

Left: Harold Cawley, MP, at Gallipoli in 1915. He wrote home, 'I keep extraordinarily well, a bit thinner, but really hard and fit.'

on the day that we had a very large mine blown up just against our trench, that the men were quite cool, everyone in his place, and ready, if there had been a Turkish attack.'

Less than a fortnight after his return to the battalion, on 24 September, Harold Cawley was killed. Like Sir Herbert Archer Croft, his eyesight was so poor he need not have volunteered for active service at all.

As winter approached the situation on the peninsula had begun to seem hopeless. On 16 October 1915, Lord Howard de Walden of Chirk Castle commenced a long letter to his young son, John. Although also a staff officer, he thought it likely enough he would 'leave my carcase out here upon this undesired cape'.

Below: Lord Thomas, 'Tommy', Howard de Walden, of Chirk Castle, (second right) at Gallipoli.

His letter is suffused with melancholy and in places full of nostalgia for his home on the Welsh borders,

'I wonder if our ghosts … will come wondering back to the grey islands of the north. I often walk in imagination as it is up the hill behind Chirk… It is all so very vivid to me, so much so that I hardly miss the very places, being content to walk that way in my own mind… I am sitting now in my room in Adams tower looking up the valley and the wind is driving the wet leaves against the panes and the fierce wind all warm and misty is booming up through those wonderful tall oaks… A dear, dear land. And I know I should be quite content to give up my life, even indirectly, for so fortunate an island.'

Evacuation

Once winter arrived it became obvious the campaign was lost. In December the troops were evacuated. Sydney Beale's mother reported to Helen on 27 December, 'They had a miserable time when they first had orders to move & had packed up their belongings when a tremendous thunderstorm & rain soaked everything & then turned cold & froze, some of the men died of it.'

The evacuation of thousands of troops under cover of night, at least, was a success. Guy Dawnay described the whole operation to his wife,

'The infantry began to withdraw. The garrison of the front trenches was left thinner, and thinner, and thinner – until at last only a few scattered snipers were left… There was no noise or confusion … and finally the snipers withdrew. All had been arranged – they came straight down to their appointed places in the dim, hazy moonlight and the silence, straight to their boats – and the last man was on the beach long before the Turks realised that the first had left the trenches. It was very wonderful…

'And so ended what so much had been endured for – so much blood shed for… No question of it being the right thing to do. We could have done no more there. Nothing could play better in the enemy's hands than to cling on stupidly to the precarious fruits of a very incomplete success.'

The men were desperately relieved to have left. One of them described events to Captain Geoffrey Wolryche Whitmore of Dudmaston Hall, who was stationed with the army in Egypt. Geoffrey passed on the information to his sister, relating, 'He says the troops cheered so when they were leaving that they were afraid the Turks would guess what was up.'

Churchill's downfall

Almost as soon as the last troops were withdrawn a government inquiry was held into the disaster, at which Guy Dawnay gave important evidence. One key document was a letter written by Harold Cawley to his father, also an MP. Sent to the House of Commons, it was not subject to censorship and was critical of almost every aspect of the campaign. It began with an attack on Sir Ian Hamilton, the Expeditionary Force's Commander-in-Chief until he was sacked in October 1915,

Left: Winston Churchill, 1915. One of his earliest paintings and a rare self-portrait which now hangs in his old studio at Chartwell.

'The curse of the whole show has been the absurd optimism of the Chief Generals particularly Ian Hamilton and Hunter Weston and the way they have underrated their opponents… the Turk is a good fighter, better at bombing than our fellows, better at digging and quite as good at sharp shooting in the trenches.'

He complained that 'the first force that came here was ludicrously inadequate' and that the initial costly attacks in April were 'often badly reconnoitred and ill conceived' observing that by the time he arrived in May 'things had pretty well settled down to trench warfare'.

Harold was full of praise for most of the British troops, saying 'The original regular 29th Division were wonderful and even with over 90 per cent of new men they are good' and he describes the Manchester Brigade as 'excellent'. He was less impressed by the Naval Division which he thought 'mostly not much' and considered the East Lancs Brigade 'bad'.

His real scorn, though, was reserved for the generals,

'Ian Hamilton lives over in Imbros and everyone curses him as a popinjay and no soldier. His chief of the staff Braithwaite is also said to be useless. Hunter Weston was a breezy optimist, a fighting man and keen but he poured out his men's blood like water without turning a hair and did not make a success of it… My other General is disliked by all his troops particularly the officers. He has a third rate brain, no capacity to grasp the lie of land and no originality or ingenuity… All the officers loathe him.'

His tirade over, Harold mentions, 'There has been a good deal of sickness mostly stomach troubles. Everyone – except myself – seems to get diarrhoea and general derangement of the insides' before concluding starkly, 'I saw my battalion yesterday; out of the original number of just over 1,000, only 61 are left.' His letter was brutal in its analysis of the complacency, lack of planning, insufficient knowledge of the terrain, disease, poor leadership and inadequate supplies that contributed to the campaign's catastrophic outcome.

As its chief architect, Churchill could not survive. Although he had had no hand in the running of the campaign, he resigned his post as First Lord of the Admiralty in disgrace. It was around this time he took up painting. One of his earliest works now hangs in his old studio at Chartwell. It is a self-portrait and shows a slight figure dressed in long white jacket, the face in half shadow, its features pained. This ghostly figure is surrounded by intense dark. It shows a man broken, in crisis. Everything was going horribly wrong.

5. LOOS, 1915

Thomas Agar-Robartes and John Kipling were very different men. They were to die within hours of one another at the Battle of Loos.

Thomas, known as Tommy, Agar-Robartes of Lanhydrock was heir to the Clifden viscountcy, a wealthy, debonair and radical Liberal MP, celebrated as 'the best dressed man in Parliament'.

John Kipling of Bateman's was still scarcely more than a boy. Only seventeen when war broke out, he was 5 foot 6 inches tall, with weak eyesight, rounded shoulders and a quiet manner. He wasn't particularly academic and didn't appear to have inherited his father's gift for words. What he shared with Tommy was a determination to the get to the Front as fast as possible.

Tommy had first been elected MP for South East Cornwall in 1906, but within a month was accused of 'the corrupt practices of bribery, treating and undue influence' and of exceeding the maximum allowed for electoral expenses.

He was disqualified, but won a new seat in 1908 and stood again in 1910 when Winston Churchill canvassed on his behalf.

Apart from his political ambitions and sporting interests, Tommy had become a lieutenant in the Royal 1st Devon Yeomanry on leaving university and when war broke out immediately joined the Royal Bucks Hussars. Once with them, he was impatient to see action and fretted about lack of opportunity. Early in 1915 he told a friend, 'I am moving Heaven and earth and using all the influence I and my family possess, to get to the front, because I want to do my bit.'

Left: Thomas Agar-Robartes. Tommy began his military career with the Royal Devonshire Yeomanry, but transferred first to the Royal Bucks Hussars and then the Coldstream Guards.

Right: Tommy as an MP. With his friend, Neil Primrose, he chose to sit among the Labour MPs. Noting this, *The Daily Chronicle* reported, 'There was something incongruous in the presence of two members always so immaculately dressed as Mr Primrose and Mr Agar-Robartes in the midst of the representatives of the industrial democracy.'

Strings pulled

John Kipling was equally determined to play his part. As soon as he turned seventeen on 17 August 1914, he was taken by his father to a local recruiting station but was turned down due to his appalling vision. He applied again, this time to the Royal Navy, but was again rejected because of deficient eyesight. Eventually and reluctantly (at least according to his wife Carrie), Rudyard appealed for help to his old friend Lord Roberts, Colonel-in-Chief of the Irish Guards. Influence won. John was commissioned as a 2nd Lieutenant.

Once in the army, he was sent to Warley in Essex which he found 'a living Hell on Earth'. Even so, Rudyard admired his son's resolve and wrote to him consolingly that discomfort was inevitable, along with a 'certain loneliness of the spirit which is awfully hard to bear; and a certain sense of isolation which, as I remember, almost frightens a young man. And you have stood it like a white man and a man to be proud of.' Just to make life a little easier, he

Above right: John Kipling as a lieutenant in the Irish Guards.

Right: John with pals (third from left). Standing on an upper step disguises the fact that he is considerably shorter than almost all his comrades.

Opposite: John with his father, Rudyard. A celebrated writer, in 1907 Kipling became the first Briton to win the Nobel Prize for Literature. It was awarded, 'in consideration of the power of observation, originality of imagination, virility of ideas and remarkable talent for narration which characterize the creations of this world-famous author.'

bought his son a little Singer motor car so he could drive up to London to visit the music halls.

Things soon changed. Ordered overseas at last, John returned home on draft leave. Rudyard had accepted work with Masterman's War Propaganda Bureau (run by writer and Head of Propaganda, Christopher Masterman) and left for France on 12 August. His son followed a few days later. Dressed in his khaki uniform, he turned to his mother on the stairs and said 'Send my love to Daddo'. Then he left Bateman's forever.

Caroline had little hope of seeing her son again and wrote, 'There is no chance John will survive unless he is so maimed from a wound as to be unfit to fight. We know it and he does. We all know it, but we all must give and do what we can and live on the shadow of hope that our boy will be the one to escape.'

France

Lady Clifden may have thought much the same as Caroline. Tommy had said a final goodbye to Cornwall and on his last journey from Lanhydrock was driven by chauffeur, Joseph Medland. His nephew, Howard, later reported, 'Uncle Joe took Tommy back to Bodmin Road station. "Goodbye, Medland," he said, "I don't think I shall be seeing you again"' – a farewell remark that left Uncle Joe thoughtful.

Tommy had transferred to the Coldstream Guards and quickly established himself as popular with his men. One of them wrote, 'What a trump Captain Robartes is! He was always extremely kind and gentle. He treated us all as friends … when he returned from leave he would immediately visit us in billets, or wherever we were, asking kindly after our welfare. Not only that, but he never returned empty-handed; a present from the homeland would be issued out to each one of us.'

Tommy had been slightly injured in May on his first tour out. For John it was all a new experience. He left England on 16 August in a ship escorted by a destroyer to protect against enemy submarines. He arrived in France on his eighteenth birthday, travelled by cattle truck towards the front and was billeted with the Mayor of Acquin whom he confided had 'a very pretty daughter – Marcelle – who is awfully nice and we get on very well'. When off duty he read copies of *Tatler* and *Punch* and ate 'topping' sponge cake sent to him by Lady Bland-Sutton. He did not have long to wait for something more serious.

A great attack was in the offing. Everyone seemed to know about it. At Abbeville where she was stationed with the Red Cross, Margaret Greg of Quarry Bank Mill noted in her diary on Thursday 23 September, 'Rumours of an advance tomorrow – more ATs (Ambulance Trains) gone up to Bethune…' and the following day, 'Great activity among ATS.

General excitement – Reinforcements and changes among Battn: to 3rd Army have been going on for weeks.'

The Battle of Loos was the only major British attack on the Western Front in 1915. It was part of a joint offensive with the French and Loos had been chosen by their Commander, Joffre. It was not suitable terrain – a scarred industrial landscape of coalmines and slag heaps and not to the liking of British Commanders Sir John French and Sir Douglas Haig.

Troop morale, though, was high. Poison gas was also to be used for the first time, while Royal Engineer tunnelling companies had laid explosive charges underground to disrupt enemy lines. At 6.30 a.m. on 25 September, British troops went over the top to the sound of bagpipes. In places their own gas blew back onto them and in others the German wire had not been broken, partly due to a shortage of ammunition that had restricted artillery preparations. Everywhere they were cut down by machine guns.

Below: The valise Tommy took with him on active service, pictured in his bedroom at Lanhydrock.

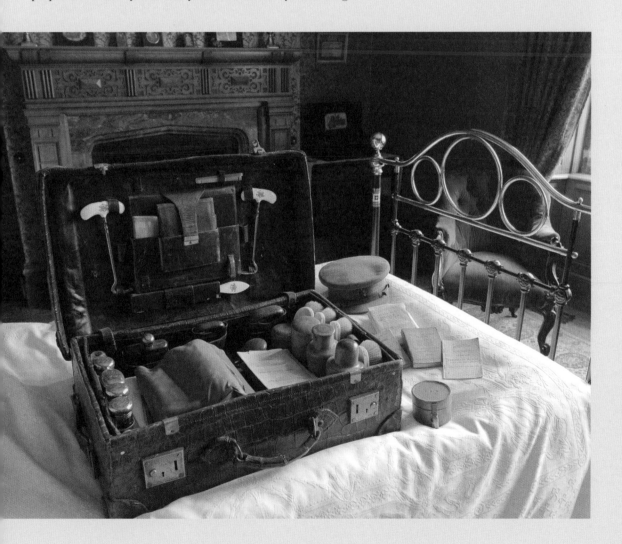

Despite these setbacks, in many places the attack was a success. Loos was taken. Reinforcements were called for to consolidate the gains, but these were too far behind the lines, took too long to move forward and as they did so were slowed by the streams of wounded leaving the battlefield. The initiative was consequently lost.

Chalk Pit Wood

Tommy and John were not yet among the casualties. John went into battle first, on 27 September. His was one of four companies of Irish Guards to attack Chalk Pit Wood, just north of Loos. As on the opening day the 'accessory', as gas was termed, was released and artillery pounded the German line. Rising from their trenches, they were met by intense shellfire but moved rapidly to the edge of the wood. In the confusion, John became caught up in a second wave attack by the Scots Guards on another objective. It was at this moment he was hit in the face and killed.

Below: John Kipling, centre, with fellow Irish Guards officers at Warley, Essex, shortly before leaving for France in 1915.

Rudyard Kipling commemorated his son's death with the couplet,

My son was killed while laughing at some jest, I would I knew
What it was, and it might serve me in a time when jests are few.

He was obviously trying to comfort himself. The reality was very different. It seems likely that most of John's face was blown off by a shell and that he was last seen stumbling in agony across the muddy battlefield. His body was never found.

Only a few hours later Chalk Pit Wood was attacked again, this time by the Coldstream Guards. Tommy was with them and it was reported that during this assault 'he walked about absolutely fearlessly and never could be persuaded to take cover of any sort. He behaved simply splendidly … his bravery was simply wonderful.'

The Coldstream Guards took and held their position. According to his Battalion Commander, it was after this that two sergeants in Tommy's company 'went out in front of trenches at the chalk pit almost up to Bois Hugo to bring in a wounded man. When they were about to return Sergt. Hopkins was shot down by a German sniper. Sergt. Printer continued on with the wounded man and brought him into our lines. Capt. Agar-Robartes, who had been watching the whole episode, at once went out wth Sergt. Printer and brought in Sergt. Hopkins, who was severely wounded. Capt. Agar-Robartes was himself fatally wounded about half an hour afterwards while superintending other rescues.'

Two of Tommy's brothers, Victor and Alexander were also at Loos. Victor noted in his diary on 28 September, 'T shot 9am. Chalk pit. Loos. Moved that night via La Routoire.' Briefly it was thought his life might not be in danger, for Sergeant Hopkins had seen him at the hospital. In a letter to Tommy's mother, he later explained, 'I could never express how I felt, while lying in Hospital and caught sight in the paper that our dear Captain had died from his wounds. I felt terrible upset for when he went down at night he was talking alright and could walk.'

Of his rescue by Tommy he wrote, 'I wanted to thank you on behalf of your gallant son … for it is to him and him alone that I have to thank you for being here today, for he came for 80 to 100 yards right across the open in broad daylight and within 200 yards of the enemy and dragged me into safety… I only know how sorry I was when a few moments afterwards he himself was brought down and layed along side of us, and although wounded as he was not once or twice but many times he asked how I was.'

Failure and loss

The battle continued, but without great hope of success. On 3 October the Germans counter-attacked and re-took some of the land they had lost. Tommy's brother Alexander was wounded in the jaw on 8 October but by then fighting was almost at an end. There was a last British assault a few days later, but when that also failed and the weather turned to rain further attacks were called off. Little ground had been gained and 59,247 British casualties had been sustained.

At Lanhydrock the servants expressed their condolences to Tommy's parents, writing, 'that we the employees of your Lordship having heard with deep regret the death of Captain Robartes desire to express our sincere sympathy and condolence with your Lordship and family in this so great bereavement.' Winston Churchill attended a memorial service for him at St Margaret's, Westminster.

Rudyard Kipling's grief for his son expressed itself through many poems. Perhaps the most powerful is 'The Children'. It begins 'These were our children who died for our lands: they were dear in our sight.' The final verse reads,

The flesh we had nursed from the first in all cleanness was given
To corruption unveiled and assailed by the malice of Heaven –
By the heart-shaking jests of Decay where it lolled on the wires –
To be blanched or gay-painted by fumes – to be cindered by fires –
To be senselessly tossed and retossed in stale mutilation
From crater to crater. For this we shall take expiation.
But who shall return us our children?

Above: Fergus Bowes-Lyon, whose family owned Gibside, Tyne and Wear. He was killed on September 27, having been involved in forty-eight hours of almost continuous combat.

Right: Letter from Sergeant Hopkins to Lady Clifden, describing Tommy's heroism; written in response to a letter from her enquiring after his health, he felt hesitant to reply to a lady of her high social status.

Lady of your rank. I think it very kind, for you to enquire after me. & I am pleased to say that my wounds are now quite healed. I left Netley Hospital on November th 19th and returned to Windsor on th 28th I was only at Windsor 8 days before comming down here and the men of Our Company thet were wounded at Loose, were just beginning to come in from the differant hospitals a few each day were turning up. but I had not up to my time of leaving windsor seen any K.C.C. return. & the men I saw I know them but, am not familiar with there names. as they were not men of my Platoon. Bergt. Pinter I have not seen n heard of since th Fatal 28 Sept. and Drill Sergt. Simonds & all the other men went away from (Hilters Clearing hospital) 4 days before me, & I had not heard of them. but may find some of them at Windsor when I get back. when they leave the Clearing stations they get taken to differant parts. I never saw another Coldstream while I was at Netley. I am going to try & get leave for Xmas. when I get back. My Address is 77 Gordon Hill (Near) Enfield Middlex London N. I could never express how I felt. while lying in hospital & caught sight in the paper. that our dear Captain had died from his wounds. I felt terrible upset for when he went down at night he was talking or right & would walk. Thanking you again for your kind enquiries.

I Remain. With deepest Symphy yars
Truly
(No 11201) Lance Bergt. A. W. Hopkins

6. THE SOMME, 1916

On 1 July 1916, 100,000 British troops climbed from their trenches and began walking across No Man's Land. By the end of the day almost 60,000 of them had been either killed or wounded. It was the single worst day in British military history. When the battle ended almost five months later, the two sides had suffered more than a million casualties between them. The Allies advanced their line by about 6 miles and claimed victory. Corporal Henry Stokoe, an estate carpenter at Wallington, was killed on that first day, serving with the Northumberland Fusiliers. His younger brother John was killed a few weeks later.

One of those who went over the top on 1 July was Captain Charles Ensor of Ardress House in Northern Ireland. He was serving with the Royal Irish Fusiliers as part of the Ulster Division. It is said that on the eve of battle one of the Ulstermen had begun to sing 'Abide with me', in a lull in the artillery bombardment. The hymn was taken up all along the trenches until shelling resumed some minutes later.

Left: Men of the Royal Irish Rifles resting in a communication during the opening hours of the Battle of the Somme, 1 July 1916.

Opposite: John Stokoe. A bright boy, he won a scholarship to grammar school. This photograph was taken to commemorate the achievement. Like his father and brother, he became a joiner at Wallington. On the outbreak of war the brothers enlisted. Henry was killed on July 1 1916, John on September 25. Henry was 28. John was 24.

Left: Henry Page Croft, MP, by Philip de Laszlo. Henry Page was on active service in France from 1914 until his return to Parliament in 1917, rising to the rank of Brigadier-General. In the inter-war period he was a keen supporter of Churchill's anti-appeasement policy and during the Second World War served as Under Secretary of State for War and as a member of Churchill's War Council, 1940-45. He was created Baron Croft in 1940 and inherited Croft Castle, Herefordshire, in 1941.

Shortly before British troops were due to leave their lines the Germans began retaliatory shellfire. At 6.25 a.m. the Royal Field Artillery began a final hour of intensive bombardment. It lifted at zero hour on a warm sunny morning. According to the 9th Irish Fusiliers' War Diary, the Battalion was deployed on a four company front; 'A' Company, on its right, was under the command of Captain Ensor. At 7.30 a.m. whistles were blown and with wild cheers and shouts the troops left their trenches.

The Ulstermen did better than any, penetrating as far as the German fourth line, but at terrible cost. Surrounded, almost out of ammunition and under fierce pressure they were obliged to withdraw. The cost had been staggering. Of the 15 officers and 615 men of the 9th Irish Fusiliers who had gone into battle, all of the officers were listed as either killed, wounded or 'missing believed killed'. Of the other ranks, 520 were dead, wounded or missing. Charles Ensor was amongst the wounded. He spent several days in No Man's Land and was eventually rescued on the night of 4 July.

Brigadier Henry Page Croft arrived at the battlefield that day. He describes the scene in *Twenty-Two Months Under Fire*. Making his way to the old British line he 'saw the first signs of the great battle, as dead horses lay in pathetic attitudes where a battery had been rushed up to support the attack'. He then, 'walked over what had been No Man's Land, ... where a hundred thousand British soldiers had charged with light heart through a rain of lead only three days before.'

Given what had happened to the Ulster Division, it might seem surprising that Henry should refer to soldiers charging with 'light heart through a field of lead' but in part this could be explained by the fact that his memoir was published in 1917. By then he was back in Parliament as a Conservative MP and he would not have wished to write anything that could be construed as defeatist or unpatriotic. His tone also reflects the fact that the troops who went over the top that first morning did so in good heart.

Kitchener's men

Morale was buoyant. The armies that had fought at Mons, Gallipoli and Loos were still largely composed of professional soldiers supported by territorial forces. The army that fought on 1 July was mostly comprised of men who had volunteered in the early days of the war in response to Kitchener's call. Many served in 'Pals' Battalions' in which friends from the same factory, sporting club, street or village had enlisted together.

Barely trained and in almost all cases without experience of war, this amateur army couldn't wait to get into action. Since 24 June they had sat through an intense bombardment during which the artillery had fired thousands of shells per day onto the German lines. No one believed the enemy could survive such punishment. All thought British troops would advance uncontested across open ground to occupy empty trenches.

Each soldier carried around 60 pounds of equipment as he went into battle, so troops were heavily encumbered as they struggled out of their trenches, but spirits would have been high. At least one officer teed off with a golf shot as the attack began and many kicked footballs into No Man's Land. They were met with streams of machine-gun fire.

In fact, the Germans occupied deep, well-constructed dugouts, often made of concrete. Once the British shelling lifted, they were able to leave their shelters and man their defensive stations. They were a formidable enemy, as Henry Page Croft was to find out on 7 July. His description of an attack on Bailiff Wood is notably more restrained in tone,

At 9.15 the Fusiliers went over the top. The Germans had turned their barrage on the valley, and it was by now a cauldron of bursting explosions. Notwithstanding these conditions the battalion advanced with perfect order, marching in quick step right through the barrage, where things looked about as ugly as possible. On they pressed until they reached a point only fifty yards south of Bailiff Wood; but here our attacking waves came under a terrible enfilade machine gun fire from Bailiff Wood and beyond... the men

*were being shot as they lay in the open, so I decided not to
throw fresh troops in.'*

Only one British Corps had been successful in taking all its initial
objectives on 1 July. Commanded by Lieutenant General Congreve, its
30th Division successfully took the key village of Montauban by 10.30
a.m. Ahead of the victorious troops lay retreating Germans. Congreve
wished to push on and telephoned for permission to do so. This
permission was denied. His orders were to capture and consolidate. As at
Loos and Gallipoli, momentum was lost.

Captain William Denman Croft arrived in Montauban only a couple of
days afterwards. William was a relative of Henry Page Croft and in a letter
written on 19 July, he recounted his experiences on the Somme to his
brother, Owen,

*'My battalion took over Montauban from a battalion of
Manchesters… They had done nothing to consolidate and
simply sat about like young rooks to get killed. That battalion*

Left: William Croft began the war with the rank of Captain and ended it as a Brigadier-General. He was one of only nine men to be awarded four DSOs (Distinguished Service Orders). He was also given the Croix de Guerre Legion d'Honneur and was mentioned in dispatches ten times.

was practically wiped out in consequence by heavy shell fire. The moment we got in we worked like hell and were fortunate enough to discover some cellars. The following morning I had patrols out in BERNAFAY wood and offered to hold it too. Bernafay wood later had to be taken by 2 battalions as the Boche got it back again.'

Phase one

Although called the 'Battle of the Somme', what took place between July and November 1916 was really a succession of battles as woods, villages and strongpoints were contested. The first phase began with the Battle of

Albert, fought between 1 and 13 July. Fighting continued with the Battle of Bazentin Ridge between 14 and 17 July. William Croft with the Cameronians was involved and described events to his brother Owen,

'We assaulted just West of Longueval village at 3:20 (Summer time) it was dark and we found the wire uncut! But the battalion attacked under heavy m.g. fire and after cutting wire got through and on our own took about a 100 prisoners after some good bombing operations.

'We reached our objective which was just West of Longueval and dug ourselves in. Snipers and m.g's simply swarmed in DELVILLE wood but I flatter myself that our trenches were as good as anything made during the war.'

Further details are added in his memoir *Three Years with the 9th Division*, published in 1919,

'The Argylls were on our right, and I shall never forget their old pipe major strutting up and down a certain well sniped road near the village, while we cowered in a ditch alongside. Someone pulled him down eventually, and his colonel sent him back to the transport lines, from which he made several attempts to get back to his battalion.

'The casualties of my battalion in that first Somme battle were over 600, and 24 officers; and the great majority took place from zero to zero plus one hour – practically at dawn. No sooner had we consolidated our line than our troubles began. At first we blazed away, with much expenditure of ammunition but with little result at fleeing Boches and snipers. It struck me pretty forcibly that there was something uncommonly like a rout in the opposition. For they were "haring" shamelessly for home, and those who were not were likewise obviously "getting their skates on". I begged and implored someone to send cavalry to complete the victory. But no doubt there were strong reasons against this course; reasons which we simple soldiers could not see, for all away up beyond High Wood were fleeing Boches.'

Yet again, the advantage of a breakthrough had not been followed up. For William, the lesson was clear, 'The employment of cavalry must be left to the man on the spot, not to the man – however great a genius he may happen to be – who sits about 20 miles back.'

Artillery

Marching towards the Somme on 16 July, General Arthur Hussey of Scotney Castle records in his memoir that he heard rumours 'of a break through by the Cavalry near Bazentin, and visions of chasing a defeated foe over open country arose, only to be shattered later by the news of the actual situation'. He had been in the area only a few months before, but found it unrecognisable,

'What a change had come over the scene! The villages of Fricourt, Mametz, and Montauban were now only heaps of debris, with a mound of white stones marking the ruins of the church in each place. Instead of a clearly defined system of trenches, with grass-land and trees in between, was a vast expanse of shell-torn ground, covered with deep, wide gashes, where trenches had once been, shattered stumps where once had been trees, and over all were scattered bombs, unexploded shells, arms, equipment, and all the other debris which marks the trail of modern battle.'

General Hussey's men took up their artillery positions on 20 July in Caterpillar Valley, which he described as 'a most "unhealthy" area. It was packed from end to end with guns of every sort, 9.2-inch, 8-inch, 6-inch, and 4.5 howitzers, 60-prs., anti-aircraft guns, and literally hundreds of 18 pr. Guns, which kept up an almost continuous roar day and night. Overlooked by the German positions at Ginchy to the East, it was made the target of much Artillery fire. There was hardly any cover for the detachments … only holes dug in the ground covered with corrugated-iron and earth, which afforded little protection.'

As if this wasn't bad enough, a couple of days later the Divisional Ammunition dump near Mametz was hit, containing 100,000 rounds of trench-mortar and artillery ammunition along with large quantities of bombs. Valiant efforts were made to extinguish the fire, 'but about half an hour after it had started it reached the trench-mortar bombs, and immediately the whole dump exploded with a tremendous detonation. Shells and bombs were hurled in all directions, and Lieut. Traill was blown about a hundred yards into the Cemetery. Luckily no one was killed, though several suffered from severe shock.'

Father and son

General Hussey went into action on the Somme on 20 July. Also involved that day was Billy Congreve, of Lindisfarne Castle. The war must have seemed very much a family affair as his father Lieutenant General Sir Walter Congreve was commanding his Division, his mother was working as a nurse in France and his twelve-year-old brother, Christopher, also turned up one day when visiting his parents. Dressed in Boy Scout uniform, he was given a tour of the trenches and is thought to have been the youngest British person to have been at the front. According to his later account, they came upon two soldiers round a traverse, one of them remarking to the other, 'Blimey, Bill – 'ere's a bleedin' Boy Scaht!'

Like his father, who had won the Victoria Cross in the Boer War, Billy had already proved himself astonishingly brave. Earlier in the year he had added a Distinguished Service Order to his Military Cross when he captured numerous prisoners at St Eloi. Following the detonation of six mines, craters had been left on the enemy-held front. In an early morning raid in darkness and fog attempts were made to secure them, but without full success. Billy arrived as dawn was breaking and thought he saw a German waving a piece of sack on a stick.

Unsure if this was a true surrender, he gathered a small party of men and approached the crater. Shots were fired at him, but he carried on in the hope the enemy would think that part of the line had already

Left: Mametz Wood, scene of bitter hand-to-hand fighting. One battalion of the Welsh Regiment attacked with 676 men. By the end of the day they had suffered 400 killed or wounded. Other battalions saw equally heavy casualties.

been taken by the British and that resistance was worthless. Reaching the rim of the crater, he peered in, later reporting,

'Imagine my surprise and horror when I saw a whole crowd of armed Boches! I stood there for a moment feeling a bit sort of shy, and then I levelled my revolver at the nearest Boche and shouted, "Hands up, all the lot of you!" A few went up at once, then a few more and then the lot; and I felt the proudest fellow in the world.'

Almost alone, Billy Congreve had taken prisoner four officers and sixty-eight men.

He continued to show such bravery on the Somme, putting himself wherever he was most needed. Since by then promoted Major, he should not perhaps have been exposing himself to unnecessary danger. 'Very wrong of him to be out on such work,' his father noted in his diary, adding 'Bless him.'

On 20 July there was again fierce fighting around Longueval. Although exhausted by lack of sleep and the strain of command, Billy was determined to assess the situation for himself. He went forward with Private Edward Roberts of the Royal Welch Fusiliers. Working their way to a disused German gun-pit, Billy used his field glasses to study enemy positions and strength, every so often pausing to make notes. As he made his way back into the main trench, he was shot in the throat. He stood for a few seconds and then collapsed dead. It was 10.55 a.m.

Right: King George V (with his back to camera, right), Generals Lord Rawlinson and Congreve, and other Staff Officers, at the grave of a British soldier; near Fricourt, August 10, 1916.

Wild flowers

News of Congreve's death reached Corps Headquarters by telephone. It fell to Brigadier-General W.H. Greenly to inform Billy's father. He did so 'at a very important and critical moment … where the direction of the corps commander was of the greatest importance. When I told him what had happened he was absolutely calm to all outward appearance and, after a few seconds of silence, said quite calmly, "He was a good soldier." That is all that he allowed to appear, and he continued dealing with everything as it came along in the same imperturbable and quietly decisive way as usual.'

Before the funeral, Lieutenant General Congreve spent a few moments with his dead son, recording,

'I saw him in the mortuary, and was struck by his beauty and strength of face… A lot of flowers were sent by kind people, amongst them wild mallows from the fighting line by some of the men. These I put into the grave… I myself put in his hand a posy of poppies, cornflowers and daisies … and with a kiss I left him.'

Above: Double image of No Man's Land, the Somme. The pictures were viewed through stereoscopic glasses to give a 3-D effect.

Left: King George V (second left) with Generals Lord Rawlinson and Congreve, inspecting a captured German trench, near Fricourt, 10th August 1916. Their guide, pointing, was Mr Harding of the Royal Engineers.

Billy's coffin was placed on an artillery gun carriage and with his father and servant, Private Cameron, as chief mourners he was buried in a cemetery overlooking the Somme valley. A short while after he was posthumously awarded the Victoria Cross for 'most conspicuous bravery'. Part of the citation reads, 'when Brigade Headquarters were heavily shelled and many casualties resulted, he went out and assisted the medical officer to remove the wounded to places of safety, although he himself was suffering severely from gas and other shell effects. He again on a subsequent occasion showed supreme courage in tending wounded under heavy shell fire.'

Bogged down

The battle continued. By the end of July 150,000 British troops had become casualties, almost double the entire Expeditionary Force that had sailed to France in August 1914. Forty thousand were dead. On 1 August Winston Churchill circulated a private paper to the cabinet criticising the High Command's tactics and advocating the attack be abandoned.

He was ignored. While at the Admiralty he had urged the development of tanks. Forty were used for the first time on 15 September but the battlefield was too torn and muddy for them to have much impact. Most became bogged down. General Arthur Hussey described an attack on the Somme assisted by tanks in his memoir, 'The 5th Division in the Great War',

'The attack on the 25th was the first occasion on which the Division was allotted "Tanks" to co-operate with the Infantry. Knowing the uncertainties of these first experimental land-ships, it was wisely decided that they should only be used to support the Infantry ... of the three Tanks allotted, one failed to start; the second proceeded some distance, but "bellied" in the mud ... whilst the third, after various vicissitudes, arrived some time after the Infantry on the South side of Morval.'

Used in greater numbers on more favourable ground, tanks might have made a decisive breakthrough. As it was, they were little more than objects of curiosity. On 12 October William Croft wrote to his mother, 'I got inside a tank yesterday,' though because of strict censorship rules, adding, 'Of course I can't describe it.'

As winter approached, the battle was finally abandoned on 18 November 1916. By this point the Allies had suffered almost 624,000 casualties, the Germans 465,000. Despite having lost more men, it was seen as an Allied victory – not least because while the British volunteers lost were bright and keen, they were inexperienced soldiers. The Germans, by contrast, had lost battle-hardened troops. This point was made by Crown Prince Rupprecht of Bavaria when he said, 'What remained of the old first-class peace-trained German infantry had been expended on the battlefield.' They had not been defeated, but they had been dealt a heavy blow.

A similar point was made by William Croft in his memoir of 1919 when he wrote,

'Our losses had been heavy – heavy even for the Somme in those early days. But, now that we can look back on it all, one feels proud to have taken part in that great offensive, the first battle of the Somme. For we gave the Boche, if not the knockout, at any rate the first dent in his armour, a dent which finally brought us victory in 1918.'

Shortly before the battle ended, on 1 November, Pamela Congreve attended a ceremony at Buckingham Palace. There she received her husband's medals, the Victoria Cross, the Distinguished Service Order and the Military Cross from King George V. No other officer had ever been awarded all three decorations. At the time she was pregnant with their only child.

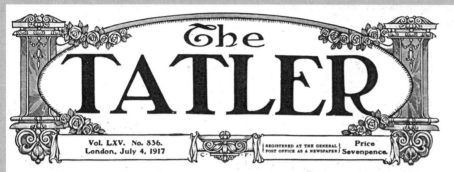

The TATLER

Vol. LXV. No. 836.
London, July 4, 1917.

REGISTERED AT THE GENERAL POST OFFICE AS A NEWSPAPER

Price Sevenpence.

Mendoza Galleries

MRS. W. LA TOUCHE CONGREVE AND HER LITTLE DAUGHTER

Mrs. W. La Touche Congreve is the widow of the late Major W. La Touche Congreve, V.C., D.S.O., M.C., who was killed in action very shortly after his marriage. He was the son of Major-General W. N. Congreve, V.C., and, like his father, was in the Rifle Brigade. Mrs. Congreve was Miss Pamela Maude and is the daughter of Mr. Cyril Maude. Her baby is a god-daughter of Queen Mary's

Left: Billy's widow, Pamela, with Mary Gloria. Their daughter was born on March 21 1917. Pamela remarried in 1919.

117

7. PASSCHENDAELE, 1917

There is only a brief entry for 9 September 1917 in the war diary of the 4th Battalion Royal Welch Fusiliers. It records the weather as 'fine' and after a short summary of what was a quiet day during the 3rd Battle of Ypres concludes, '1 OR Killed in Action'. The 'Other Ranks' killed was Private Frederick Hughes.

Fred Hughes was born on the Chirk Castle estate in 1897. His father died young, leaving a widow to bring up five children in a three-room cottage. Fred tried hard as a child to help the family, collecting firewood for the bread oven, scavenging pieces of coal from the colliery slag heap and growing food in the garden. He left school when he was fourteen to begin work down the pit and at fifteen he lied about his age to join the local Territorials. The first time he ever left home was to a training camp in Aberystwyth in July 1914. While there, Fred was mobilised along with

Below: Allied troops at the Yser Canal, Belgium, 31 July 1917. The opening day of the Third Battle of Ypres (Passchendaele).

everybody else. He gave all of his £5 mobilisation allowance to his mother. By November 1914 he was in France.

Fred's earliest letters home have been lost. Those that survive begin in March 1915, the majority written to his younger brother, Edward (Ted). They present a picture of a man who in many ways seems like the archetypal Tommy – stoical, good humoured, undemonstratively patriotic and bound by intense loyalty to his comrades.

Food and cigarettes were a regular feature of his correspondence and a typical comment reads, 'The mince pies were in the pink and I was glad of the fags.' Food packages supplemented army rations and provided reminders of home. Only a few days before his death, Fred wrote to Ted on 27 August 1917, 'I received your most welcome letter and parcel quite safe for which I thank you very much. My pal and I were sitting down in a dugout wondering what we were going to have for tea; we had two Army Biscuits between us. My pal said, "Fred, I wish someone would send us a parcel", and not half an hour later the orderly Corporal came and brought the two of us a parcel.'

Much earlier, on 16 May 1915 he had written, 'Thank you for the parcel and letter … I don't think I ever enjoyed a bit of cake, and a suck of lemon better in my life. It was a feast. We have been living on biscuits for over a week, so you may guess what the cake was like to us. I say us because there are six of us in our mess, and we share everything with one another.'

Army life

Sharing with mates was obviously a fact of army life and after Fred's death Private Benjamin Butterman mentioned in his letter of condolence, 'There was a parcel arrived here for him on the day he was killed, and we thought it useless to return it knowing that it would only get spoiled on the way, so we shared it between us. We hope we have not done wrong by doing so.'

The communality of life in the army obviously appealed to Fred. In letters from April and June 1916 he wrote, 'Its Sunday morning now, and there are a gang of chaps in the corner of the hut, we are singing Welsh and it sounds grand. I have spoken more Welsh myself since I've been out here than what I did at home… If you was in our hut now you would enjoy yourself better than being at any Hippodrome, Picture Palace, or Concert; you have never seen such a cheerful happy go lucky fellows in all your life. Well I cant write much more as it is up to me to sing next.'

Fred's sense of companionship was clearly reciprocated. After his death, several of his mates wrote letters of condolence. Private Butterman said 'all the boys out of his platoon loved him very much… Your son and I, were in the Batt choir, and whenever there was any duty to be done we

did it both together. I am very sorry to lose such a good and true pal.'
Sergeant Jack Harris lamented 'I have lost the best pal I ever had' while
Lance Corporal Edward Evans described himself as 'Fred's best chum'
saying, 'He was a fine fellow and always carried a cheery disposition… He
was in my section, my bed mate, and work mate. He was clearly loved by
everyone that he came into contact with, and I can assure you that it has
upset us all very much to lose him, but lets hope that we shall all meet
again in that land of no sorrow.'

Death was an unavoidable part of life and the loss of friends is
regularly mentioned in Fred's correspondence, though one incident seems
to have troubled him more than most, since it was referred to in three
successive letters on 7, 8 and 9 June 1915 in almost identical terms, 'We
have been called up to the trenches again after two days rest, and we have
lost a few more men. Lloyd Jones from the Vron has been killed, and a
man from the Rhos was killed right by me…' 'Lloyd Jones from the Vron
has been killed; he had the back of his head right off…' 'Lloyd Jones from
the Vron has been killed, and a man from the Rhos was killed right by me.'

These were men from the community in which Fred had grown up.
The cottage where he was born was just off the Holyhead Road, two miles
from Chirk, near Pontcysyllte, known as Vron and not far from Llangollen
and Rhosllanerchrugog, known as Rhos. His officer was also local and
wrote of Fred, 'I am proud that Vron produced such a fine man. I come
from Llangollen myself, so looked on him as a man from my native town.'

Home thoughts

In one of his last letters to Ted, on 20 August 1917, Fred reminisced
about harvests as a child, 'We are having lovely weather here now, and its
fine to see the acres and acres of corn etc. that are waiting to be carried in;
it makes me think of the time you and I used to run after the waggons at
Plas Offa Farm for a ride, and of the happy times we used to have then;
but did we think they were happy moments then? No! we were either
grumbling or fighting, and I was mostly to blame. What would I give to
have those happy times over again, its like I heard a Chaplain say, "that no
one can taste the fullness of joy and happiness unless they have
experienced some sorrow or trouble."'

Despite all the dangers and discomforts, Fred was uncomplaining. He
only returned home to Britain twice after embarking for France in 1914.
The first time was that winter, when repatriated with frostbite and again
late in 1916 when he was hospitalised with a leg wound. Leave was almost
an impossibility, but he was determined to carry on. In August 1916 he
wrote that the soldiers in France 'will have the consolation of knowing
that we have done our duty to the land that gave us birth' and in the same

letter remarked, 'I dont think I was made for a soldier, but I shall feel it my duty to remain one as long as my country needs me; and I shall have the consolation of coming home with the smile of victory on my face, knowing that I have not played the coward's part.'

In common with many others, Fred knew he was in for a long war. In December 1915 he told Ted, 'You have got hopes of seeing me before Christmas. I daresay you might see me before Christmas, but I dont know which it might be. 1920 or sometime in the next century, but you know the old saying, "Better late than never".'

Water and sludge

Fred Hughes was resigned to seeing things through. In midsummer 1916 he wrote, 'What sort of weather are you having

Above: The miseries of trench warfare, 1917: shells, mud, water, gas. Image from the Croft family archives.

around home. Its awful here, rain, rain, rain and nothing but rain, and it is cold with it. More like November than June. The trenches are full of water and the roads are full of sludge and muck; but for all that we are still the happy go lucky fellows we are rightly called. The more trying our ordeals the happier we are.' He was just as chirpy in the appalling conditions of Ypres, writing on 27 August, 'we are having some awful weather, but it doesnt daunt us; we're just as happy when we are up to our knees in mud as what we are when we are in a cushy billet miles behind the line.'

Fred was in a labour battalion. This meant that while other soldiers took turns on sentry duty or patrolling No Man's Land, his job was to rebuild trenches and repair communication lines. As he put it in a couple of letters in 1915, 'I am working nights now, but am expecting to go days soon; we are digging trenches and making dugouts and all sorts of jobs in which the pick and shovel are concerned… We are having a pretty rough time of it out here, the nights are getting very cold, and dark early, and as we do all our work in the dark, we get plenty of work and very little rest, but we don't grumble, we make ourselves feel as happy and as merry and bright as possible.'

It was unheroic work, but vital. Both Arthur Hussey and William Croft commented on men like Fred when recounting Passchendaele in their memoirs. As Brigadier Hussey put it, 'Throughout our stay here, the Divisional Engineers and Pioneers worked night and day in repairing and improving this and the other roads, overcoming tremendous difficulties in the way of mud, and generally under shell-fire; and their work in maintaining tracks in the forward area (in doing which they had numerous casualties) in a great measure rendered success in the front line possible. To them must be given a large share of the honours of the battle.'

On his way up to battle through the Flanders mud, William Croft was equally grateful, 'There were only two lines of approach for the whole brigade... These two lines of approach to our assembly positions consisted of duckboard tracks, which led all the way from the canal bank to beyond St Julien. How we blessed the noble men who had performed that splendid work.'

When the end came for Fred, on 9 September 1917, it was not in a dramatic charge or with an act of selfless bravery. Lance Corporal Evans gave an account to Fred's mother, saying he 'was killed this morning by shrapnell from a bursting shell whilst out working behind the lines... He was killed instantaneously, being wounded in two or three places in the stomach; they were slight, but fatal, and he died with a loving smile on his face.'

Much the same account was given by a Sergeant Harris, who told her, 'He was killed with his face toward the enemy by a splinter of shell which fell not so far from where the boys were working; he was buried with as much respect as possible, and a wreath, and also a wooden cross marks the spot where he is buried.' Fred was two months short of his twentieth birthday which tragically was not unusually young.

Friends in high places

Fred had fought at both Loos and on the Somme. By contrast with those, the battlefield of Ypres was of British choosing, against the advice of senior French generals and without the backing of David Lloyd George and Winston Churchill. This counted for little. Winston was on the back benches and still tainted by the failure of Gallipoli. David Lloyd George was Prime Minister but head of a coalition dominated by Conservatives who supported Field Marshal Sir Douglas Haig. More importantly, Haig was a personal friend of King George V. It proved politically impossible to stop the offensive.

He had chosen Ypres as the point of attack in part in the hope that he could smash through German lines to the coast, cut off their rail communications and then assault their positions from the flank and rear.

He also argued he could at the same time close the ports of Zeebrüge and Ostend to enemy U-boats. Whatever the soundness of this plan, there were severe arguments against it, not least the fact the German lines at that point were formidably defended with a series of concrete fortifications and that the British line bulged towards it. This meant they were exposed to fire from the sides as well as ahead.

Most critically, opponents of the offensive argued the ground was unsuitable. Flanders is almost all low-lying ground of heavy clay. It had been drained over centuries by an intricate system of dykes and ditches. These had been smashed by shellfire from both sides and unseasonably heavy rain meant that the battlefield quickly flooded. In a letter of 4 August, Fred wrote to his brother about the 'absolutely rotten weather' saying 'it started to rain the 31st of July, and up to the time of writing it hasn't stopped, the place is like a sea of liquid mud.'

Above left: Adrian Drewe, by Louisa Starr Canziani. Born in 1891, Adrian studied medicine at Cambridge but joined the artillery rather than the RAMC. He took great interest in the building of Castle Drogo but was killed before its completion.

Above: Adrian was killed at Ypres in the build-up to the battle on 12 July 1917. His sister recalled that, 'after my brother Adrian's death…the joy of life went out of life as far as my father and mother were concerned… my father really was somewhat of an invalid afterwards.'

Messines Ridge

Echoing Fred's words, William Croft described conditions in his memoir, 'the ground was water-logged owing to incessant rain, and since everything was pitted with deep shell-holes it was a matter of the greatest difficulty to get along at all, even if you were completely fit and fresh. It tired you completely by the time you had done half a mile.'

Haig's timing was unfortunate. He had hoped to begin the battle earlier in the year, but agreed to postpone it while the French carried out a separate offensive further south. This failed, but crucially delayed British plans. Activity only began on 7 June with a preliminary attack on Messines, which opened with the detonation of nineteen mines beneath enemy defences. These simultaneous explosions were so loud, it is said they could be heard in Downing Street and caused the instant death of 10,000 Germans.

Involved in the attack was a young artillery officer, Felix Brunner, later of Greys Court. In a letter home he wrote, 'At five minutes past three the sky to the east became suddenly red and the earth shook several times. Mines were exploding. At ten past three the guns opened up and the infantry went over. We put up a shrapnel barrage firing first on the front line and lifting gradually to the top of the ridge. The barrage lasted 100 minutes. The ridge was then in our hands.'

The ridge Felix referred to ran north east from Messines to Passchendaele. Although only 80 metres above sea level, it commanded surrounding terrain and its capture was a rare British success. Quite why Haig did not follow this up immediately is unclear, but it was not until 31 July that he attempted to take the north part of the ridge.

Defence in depth

Delay had given the Germans opportunity to strengthen their position against an assault they knew to be inevitable. The situation faced by the British was described in his memoir by Arthur Hussey,

'The Germans had now ... organised a defence in depth. The forward area was held by an irregular line of fortified and garrisoned shell-holes, supported by concrete strongpoints. This "Mebus" or, as it was generally known, "Pill-box" was a rectangular "dug-out" of anything up to 20 feet square, built of re-inforced concrete 3 feet or more in thickness, and proof against direct hits of shells of 6-inch or even larger

Right: German-pill box, 1917.

124

calibre. In each of these forts was a garrison armed with one or more machineguns fired through long, narrow loopholes. They were sited irregularly in the position, so as to cover all the ground with their fire and so break up the lines of our attacking Infantry. Being invulnerable to rifle and machine-gun fire, except through the loopholes, the only way in which they could be reduced was for the loopholes to be kept under fire, while a party armed with bombs crept forward, surrounded the "Pill-box," and either killed the garrison or forced them to surrender by bombing through the loopholes or doorway .'

Above: Medical orderlies on the Western Front. Of their work at Passchendaele, Arthur Hussey wrote, 'The carry for stretcher-bearers over the boggy, shell-swept ground… was extremely long and arduous... The devotion to the wounded displayed by the Medical Officers and the RAMC personnel was of the highest order; their casualties were heavy.'

Right: Thomas Riversdale Colyer-Fergusson, VC.

To overcome a pill-box, therefore, attackers had to advance against machine-gun fire and then push a phosphorous bomb through the screen placed over the embrasure or kick down the door and throw in grenades.

Riversdale

This was the kind of prospect faced on the first day of battle by Thomas Riversdale Colyer-Fergusson, VC, of Ightham Mote in Kent. Educated at Harrow, he joined the army straight from school in 1914, rather than take up a place at Oxford. He received his commission in February 1915. One of his letters to survive was written to his siblings in January 1917. It deals with the routine discomforts of army life in a rest area, 'Last night some aeroplanes came and dropped bombs quite close and made a frightful row which disturbed us so much that I played bridge frightfully badly and lost six shillings before they went away… The weather is very bad again and the hut we are in leaks slightly over my bed so I shall not be sorry when we go back again.'

Serving with the 2nd Battalion, Northamptonshire Regiment, he was part of an attack at the southernmost point of an 8-mile front. An account of his actions was later given in *The London Gazette* in September. It states that, 'the tactical situation having developed contrary to expectation… and owing to the difficulties of the ground and to enemy wire, Captain

Colyer-Fergusson found himself with a sergeant and five men only. He carried out the attack nevertheless, and succeeded in capturing the enemy trench… During this operation, assisted by his orderly only, he attacked and captured an enemy machine gun… Later, assisted only by his sergeant, he again attacked and captured a second enemy machine gun.' According to the battalion diary, it was

'while directing the consolidation Captain T.R. Colyer-Fergusson was killed by a sniper. He had done magnificently. The capture of Jacob Trench was largely due to his courage and initiative.' For his 'amazing record of dash, gallantry and skill' Riversdale was awarded a posthumous Victoria Cross. He was twenty-one years old.

Wheel to wheel

To enable advancing troops to have any chance against the heavily defended German lines, the artillery had developed the creeping barrage in which shells were fired in an area slightly ahead of the attackers to suppress enemy response. Lessons had been learned from the struggle in the Somme and artillery was seen as key to success. There was no longer a shortage of ammunition and there were fewer dud shells. Regarding this improved situation, Felix Brunner had exclaimed just before Messines, 'we now fire sometimes as much in 24 hours as we did in 3 weeks when I first came out.'

Not only was there more ammunition, there were also more guns than ever before, with over 3,000 drawn up for the battle, positioned wheel to wheel. This density of firepower involved many logistical problems, not least that of supply. Arthur Hussey vividly described the difficulties,

'Some of the Artillery ammunition was taken forward by light railway, which was always being broken up by shells, but most of it and the Infantry supplies were sent up on pack mules or horses. It was possible for Transport to be got fairly far forward in some places on the plank roads, but as these were constantly under shell-fire, and frequently smashed up, wagons rarely made the journey without becoming bogged at one point or another—with consequent delay.'

Apart from hampering supply, the depth of mud meant that withdrawing batteries had to leave their guns in situ for the relieving gunners, since they were stuck fast and impossible to move. William Croft sympathised, 'The gunners had the hell of a time all through, but never worse than at

Passchendaele. With their guns axle-deep in mud and with heavy casualties among their layers.'

Although lessons had been learned from the Somme, the gloomy pattern was repeating. Limited ground was gained, but always at huge cost. The big breakthrough never came.

Slogging on

Even before the battle started, Winston Churchill had been keen to limit British losses. He felt that without clear evidence the attack was succeeding, it should be abandoned.

In truth, there was a terrible logic to pushing on with the battle. By 7 October there was a strong argument for the British to retreat to a defensible line, but that would have meant conceding ground gained at the cost of more than 200,000 casualties. That would have looked like defeat. Haig pushed doggedly forward.

Writing to his father-in-law, Lord St Oswald, of Nostell Priory, Guy Westmacott questioned how much longer things could continue. Of the conditions he wrote on 3 September, 'This place bears no description whether you are in the line or just out you get shelled to hell all day and most of the night.' Of enemy planes he said, they 'are very active and they fly quite low over us and loose off their machine guns at us so life … is not much fun. We've got a lovely day today but it has been awful – blowing and raining intermittently and darned cold at night. How nice it must be at Nostell and I've often longed to be back there. I can't conceive that this will continue after this year at this intensity. I think human nature is reaching the limit of its endurances and every body will try and make some arrangement this winter.'

The battle continued even though many rifles were so choked with mud they could not be used. William Croft attacked on 12 October and gave an account in his memoir,

'The Highlanders took over the battle front forty-eight hours before zero hour. Consequently they had to stand up to their knees in half-frozen mud, chewing the cud of their own reflections; for they had nothing else to do, being shelled freely and often… Of course the Boche knew we were going to attack. He realised perfectly well that we must get on to the ridge before winter: that we could never sit where we were in that unspeakable swamp…

'The people on our left were simply waterlogged, and no

progress made. The Argylls made a most gallant effort across the Lekkerboterbeek, in which many of them drowned … the day following we were able to advance our line by taking several pill boxes … but our casualties! For the two brigades it must have been well over 2,000 and so many of them killed … owing to the flooded shell holes it was an odds on chance a wounded man would be drowned. Poor Johnson of the 11th was a case in point.'

It was hellish, and the names given to the battered points in a devastated landscape tell their own story… Suicide Corner, Dead Dog Farm, Idiot Cross-Roads, Stinking Farm, Dead Horse Corner, Shelltrap Barn, Hellfire Cross-Roads.

Mud, mud, mud

The battle was finally ended on 7 November. By then the British had sustained 300,000 losses for the gain of 2,000 yards. The bodies of 90,000 men were never found. The names of 54,986 of these are commemorated at the Menin Gate. This stands at the end of the Menin Road, down which so many soldiers marched to their death. It was described by Arthur Hussey as 'littered on either side with debris and dead horses, was at all times blocked by Transport, was constantly under shell-fire, and was subject to aeroplane bombing and machine-gun attacks by day and night.'

He ends his account of the battle with the words, 'The remaining impression is MUD! MUD! MUD! and shell-fire' and says it was fought 'under the most appalling difficulties which had ever faced an Army'. It is alleged that when Haig's Chief of Staff, Lieutenant General Sir Launcelot Kiggell finally visited the fighting zone at Passchendaele he burst into tears and exclaimed, 'Good God, did we really send men to fight in that?'

Once the Germans began their spring offensive the following year, all of the high ground the British army had battled so hard to win in 1917 was conceded within a few days, almost without a fight.

Above: Stretcher bearers struggling through the mud near Boesinghe, August 1, 1917.

Left: British troops attack a German machine-gun post, Polygon Wood, east of Ypres, September 1917.

8. SOLDIERING ON: EVERYDAY LIFE ON THE WESTERN FRONT

More than 6 million men served with the British forces in the First World War. Precise figures are unclear, since many army records were destroyed during the Blitz. All these men had to be provisioned with food, clothing and ammunition, trained, transported, medically treated when wounded and buried when dead – if there was any body left to bury. It is said that during the war almost 7,000 miles of railway tracks were laid in France to facilitate troop movements; that 137,224,141 pairs of socks were issued, 75 million Mills bombs were thrown between 1915 and 1918, and that each army division required 30 tons of forage per day to feed its horses.

At the bottom of this vast organisation was the private soldier. 'A private doesn't get looked on as any class', wrote Fred Hughes somewhat glumly in July 1915. Men like him generally came from poor backgrounds and he was constantly hard up. After a two-day train ride in June 1917, he was again in uncharacteristically low spirits, complaining, 'Horse trucks are not very comfortable things to ride in, and to make matters worse I'd never been so poor in all my life. I never even had a fag end or the means of getting any.'

Short of money himself, Fred worried about how much the parcels sent to him cost his family. In May 1915 he wrote to his brother Ted, 'I should like you to send me a packet of Cocoa, and a few lumps of sugar, but I don't want you to go to any expense you know. I left four or five shillings in the cupboard, you can spend that on my behalf' and in July he cautioned, 'Don't send any parcel unless you can afford it, because I don't enjoy them when I know you are sacrificing yourself for me.'

Harold Hepworth, son of the gamekeeper at Nostell Priory felt the same, writing to his wife Peg in April 1916, 'I must thank you very much for being so kind and for thinking of me so much but lovie you must not spend so much money on me, darling it must cost you so much for my parcels.' They didn't always arrive in prime condition and in the same letter he had to tell her, 'I am sorry to say the last but one was damaged the bottle of sauce was broken.' Fred had similar experiences, requesting Ted, 'When you send another parcel would you mind putting a piece of paper or something between the chocolate and the cake. I had a job to tell which was which last time, but I enjoyed them alright.'

Trench life

Whatever their social background, all soldiers faced the common conditions of trench life – shells, rats, cold and lice. Billy Congreve noted in his diary on 8 September 1915, 'We found the trenches in an awful state … and the rats made me feel horrid, like wanting to be sick. However, they reduce the bodies to skeletons fairly quickly – such rats they are, big as rabbits, and so bloated that they hardly take the trouble to run.' Fred felt very much the same. Writing from 'some desolated part of Flanders' to Ted in March 1916 he told him, 'We are billeted in a barn and when we get down to it at night, and blow out the lights, you should see the rats, or rather feel them walking over your face; it makes me shudder to think about them. I would rather see a Boche coming towards me than a rat.'

Like rats, lice were a constant aggravation. In June 1915 Fred requested Ted send him a football sweater as shirts had 'too many seams' in which the lice could lay their eggs. A couple of months later he commented that 'we sweat and then start to cool down, then things in our

Left: William Croft, centre, with fellow Cameronians in January 1915. They are dressed for a winter in the trenches, having adopted a stray dog as recruit.

shirts, trousers and coat come crawling out, and we almost scratch ourselves away.' Officers were not immune, William Croft telling his brother Owen in December that year, 'I am lousy. I don't mind it but it prevents me from sleeping. The lice are as big as bumblebees and bit me on the bum and honestly it felt like a sting of a wasp.'

Freezing temperatures were another problem, the war years coinciding with some of the coldest winters of the century. In 1915 Fred had asked for 'that sleeping helmet I had out here last winter. It is getting very cold now. If it gets much colder I shall be having another dose of frostbite.'

Things were not much better for Harold Hepworth in February 1917. He wrote to tell Peg, 'I know I am nearly frozen hard every morning, and I have such a bad cold and cough.' Remembering that cold winter more than fifty years later, an old comrade reminded Felix Brunner, 'We shared a small hut together and slept on the floor in our sleeping bags. One morning when I awoke I found that I could not move my head, for during the night the moisture of my breath had frozen my chin to the blankets. You saved the situation by chipping away the ice and setting my head free.'

Shell shocks

Shellfire was another constant danger. In June 1915 Fred wrote that 'Fritz keeps throwing his old iron factories at us all the while, and a few of them come a lot too close to be pleasant; the beastly things have made my watch stop with their rotten concussions, but I have got it to go again after a lot of coaxing.' A month later Billy Congreve noted in his diary, 'The Germans started with the big *Minenwerfer*. This is a beast – about 12 inches in diameter and 2 foot 6 inches long, range about 700 yards. The first thing I knew about him was when I heard him coming. I looked up and saw him. He looked quite innocent. "Wuff, wuff, wuff," he said. Then he steadied himself and came straight down. A moment's pause, then the most almighty big bang ... it was the nastiest thing to see and I could not help wondering when or where the next was coming.'

As well as the danger of direct hits and shrapnel, there was the added risk of trenches collapsing under shellfire. This happened to William Croft during the Battle of Arras in 1917. He was in a 'tiny shaft about 8 feet down' when an 8-inch shell exploded above, killing eleven men, blasting two wounded men into the dugout and burying them all. In his memoir he recalled, 'How I thanked God that I had insisted on having a pick and shovel in that shaft, for I had been buried before. The air grew more stuffy every minute, and at last we had to put the light out as we were gradually suffocating.'

After much digging a small air hole was created and as William 'was the smallest of the three unwounded men, I was pushed up to try my luck at

Right: An explosion at St Eloy. The original caption to the picture reads, 'The Huns blow up the last bridge and isolate our hard-pressed battalions.'

getting out... Then I felt something warm and very wet. Working on with feverish energy I crawled through yet another of these warm and liquid somethings, and then out into God's pure air.' What he had crawled through was the corpses of the men killed in the explosion.

Weapons of war

The war generated all kinds of other new and horrible ways to die. One of these was the German *flammenwerfer*, first used at the 2nd Battle of Ypres in July 1915. In August, Billy came across one 'in a sort of cupboard, let

On the Battlefield.

New Soldier (pointing to the observation balloon):
"What's them in the air mate?"
Veteran: "Why don't cher know?"
"Them's canteens for aeroplanes?"

J. W. Stonelake.
R.A.M.C.
12.2.18.

into the side of the trench and was in perfect condition and complete. It is full of the most filthy stinking sort of tar stuff.' Designed to be carried by a single man, it used pressurised air and carbon dioxide or nitrogen to project a stream of burning oil 18 yards forward, 6 feet wide at its crown.

An even greater danger was gas. Introduced by the Germans in January 1915, tear gas was followed by chlorine, phosgene and mustard. It would sink to the bottoms of shell holes into which men crawled, poison the water they drank, and cause terrible suffering and horrible death. William recounts the night before an attack at Passchendaele in his memoirs, in which 'the Boche started on us with gas. As it was pitch dark it was impossible to march in our gas masks, since one could only with difficulty stay on those treacherous boards even in daylight. So we were forced to let the gas do its worst on our eyes, just keeping the tubes between our lips.' Once in position in an 'insecure pill-box' packed with men, he then had to sit in his gas mask 'the whole of that night – a good preparation for fighting at dawn!'

Fred Hughes was philosophical about the new technology of war. Writing to Ted in one of his last letters home he said, 'as the war grew older it was essential for us to create devices to kill, in order to have the upper hand of our enemy. We did not want to do it, it was a case of "we had to do it".'

At rest

Soldiers were most obviously in danger when in the front line, but in a division of 20,000 men, only 10 per cent would be at the front at any one time. The others would be either in support (in the second line of trenches) or in reserve (further back, but still near at hand in the event of emergency). When in the latter Fred wrote to Ted in August 1915, 'we are in the trenches, in reserve. We have been in the front line for a week, we were not far off the Germans; they used to shout "Go away John Bull", "England no good", but we let them know whether we are any good or not. We dropped a few tons of bombs on them and they haven't shouted "English no good" since.'

Once out of the line, troops would be at rest, though as Fred was keen to point out to Ted in an undated letter of 1916, 'We have been in, or up against the line this last two months or so … but I'm not grumbling, as a matter of fact I'd have soon as be up in the line as "resting". In civil life the word resting means having an easy time of it, but not so in the Army; here it means tiresome drills, long route marches, cleaning, brushing, polishing and endless other things that make one wish that La Gurre was over. Well Old lad, I think I'll have to close now, as its almost time to put our packs on to get to the trenches to work.'

Left: Page from an autograph book belonging to Amy Bates who nursed at Clandon Park. Some of the drawings have been carefully produced and must have provided patients with a valuable distraction.

If life at rest had its downsides, there were compensations. Not least was the chance to get clean, as Fred indicated in a letter in June 1915, 'When we are near the trenches we bathe in brooks and streams; but when we are resting, we go to a proper bath and have a good one. There is a canal near us twenty feet deep, so we dont do too bad for a wash, only short of a bit of carbolic soap.'

Whether in the line or at rest, there was always slack time that had to be filled. One simple pleasure was smoking. Fred didn't smoke before he went to France, but he found 'when you are in the trenches or on guard a smoke eases the mind and helps to pass the monotonous hours away'. Another distraction was reading. In June 1915 Fred wrote to Ted, 'I was very pleased to have the Union Jack once again in my hands; as soon as I started to read it everybody wanted to know what paper I'd got, I think about twenty read that paper so dont forget to send it again next week.'

Letters home

One important way to fill the time was letter writing. There were though, frustrations, since the letters of the private soldiers were censored. Fred clearly wanted to write more than he was allowed, complaining, 'I cannot say what I would like to say … because the censor is so beastly strict; its the hardest thing in the world to try and write a letter here, we have got to keep to the same old subject, "I am quite well and how are you etc." its very annoying, but I suppose it cant be helped.'

To an extent, the censorship was inevitable, but soldiers resented the intrusion. This was something Harold Hepworth, from Nostell Priory, mentioned several times, such as in July 1917 when he said, 'I don't like writing a lot when our officers have them to censor' or on another occasion 'I know my letters are rather cold at times lovie but you never know who is going to read them darling' and in a missive around the same time he told her, 'if the censor gets hold of this letter he will think I have gone mad.'

It was naturally assumed unnecessary to censor officers' letters, since they could be relied upon not to give away strategic information. Alan Dawnay, brother of Guy Dawnay of Beningbrough Hall, was aware of this when he wrote from France in September 1914, 'It occurs to me that this letter may be rather censorable in parts – but as I am my own censor, I must take responsibility for anything that may be open to criticism.'

Soldiers were allowed to post two free letters a week, but wrote many more. Fred had written three, to his mother, sister and cousin, on the day he died. Extra postage was obviously needed, though he struggled to find the stamps, writing in May 1916, 'I am still at a loss as to how to get a French Red Cross stamp. I've asked a few hundred people, but its all (No Compry) don't understand, or (Nappo Finny) Finished.'

He also had to find stamps when he sent home a souvenir since 'they wont let me send it without me spending some postage on it'. Some of the relics seem trivial, like a 'ring made out of a German shell nose, and part of a German button' but others have a ghoulish quality. After Loos he sent home a box of things he'd found near Hill 70. They were brought by a comrade returning on leave and included 'a small note book, also a wrist watch. It only needs a new glass and a finger on it. It goes alright. I took it off a dead Scotchman's hand. There is a knife, two razors, a belt with some cap badges, and some buttons… Just share them round the best way you think, but give Mamie and Sally those RWF [Royal Welch Fusiliers] cap badges, and a few buttons.'

Above: Page from autograph book belonging to Amy Bates. Many entries in the autograph book reflect regimental or national pride.

THE MAN WHO SPILT THE RUM

Above: Page from Amy Bates' autograph book. Several of the contributions to the book show a high level of artistic competence, as well as humour.

In the pink

Letters sent home from active service were always valued, partly for the information they contained, but also for the knowledge that at least at the time of writing the sender was 'in the pink' (meaning in good health). Since considered good for troop morale, a huge effort went into providing men with their post – 12 million letters crossing the Channel every week. It is estimated that 7,000 sacks of mail were delivered daily, being sent up to the front line with the rations.

Along with the sacks of mail, 60,000 parcels a day were also delivered. Fred Hughes was ever appreciative, writing in an undated letter of 1915, 'The parcel came at the right time, when we had nothing for tea after a twelve mile march in full marching order so you can tell we felt pretty hungry, and the parcel was most acceptable.' Harold Hepworth was no less grateful, telling Peg in June 1916, 'The socks were champion just what I wanted I have been wet through this last 6 days and they were just right and nice and warm.' Even Brigadier Generals expressed similar gratitude, Arthur Hussey writing to his sister, Gertrude in January 1918, 'I have never yet written to thank you for the slippers, which arrived about a week ago. They are nice and warm and most acceptable.'

The language used often belongs to a distant age. Writing thanks for a parcel in June 1915, Fred told Ted, 'The Apricots and Welsh bread and butter was spiffing.' He continued, 'Our mess had quite a feast. Well Dear Brother we are resting, and have been over a week. We are in a grand place and are enjoying ourselves champion. We have concerts every night, and there has been a boxing contest on; we have seen some grand boxing. We have a bath every day in a swimming bath, so we are in the pink till we go up to the trenches again.'

Sporting times

This last letter shows that being at rest wasn't always as bad as Fred had earlier suggested. It also shows the importance of sport. If the Victorians hadn't invented sports, they had at least codified their rules and developed leagues and competitions. By the early 1900s many British men of all classes were obsessed with games of every kind. The army encouraged this as a way of occupying the men's time, building morale and of course keeping them fit.

Even when up the line, Fred told Ted in April 1916, 'we have a football match nearly every day with different regiments, we have beat the RFA-RAMC. 15 8th and 7th London's so you can see we have a bit of sport sometimes.' Some of the recreations were more informal, and later in the year he wrote to say, 'it has been snowing all day today, its the first fall of snow I've seen this winter, and of course being down at rest, we had a snow-balling match with the 19th and 20th London Regiment Bombers, and we didn't half make them go.'

The upper classes were equally happy to indulge. At rest at Etricourt in 1917, Victor Agar-Robartes and chums played 'Eton football' in which, according to his diary, an over-enthusiastic Monkey 'paid the penalty by getting the whole bully on top of him and put his knee out. Colonel Follett in goal.'

Gentlemen at war

Victor faced the same dangers as Fred and was a brave man. He was wounded three times and received the Military Cross, but in many ways he seems to have regarded the war as a huge lark. One diary entry in 1917 reads, 'the Ladies of the house having lent valuable assistance, an excellent meal is provided. A piano is secured from Ernie Platt and largely contributes to the success of "Kidney Wiper", tastefully rendered by Mackay. "Bouquet et baiser" tableau! After an excess of etiquette amongst the musicians the meeting settles down to a session at "roll-ball". Stock's virgin attempt succeeds nicely to the tune of --- after which he retires to bed. Ernie refuses to sing "Bullocky Bill".'

Christmas Day 1915 had been equally uproarious, for after a church service in the morning it had been 'devoted to feasting, drinking and telling stories … to bed about 1 a.m. Alas some of the party find their beds slightly on the move and Desmond only averts a tragedy by consuming chocolate peppermints. This proceeding causes much interest among the older school of drinkers. Rouse presents his compliments to the moat later on.'

That Christmas Day had been shared in different ways by William Croft and Billy Congreve. William described his in a letter to his brother, Owen, 'On Xmas day there was a tacit truce between the enemy and our end and I hear everywhere else. The men left their trenches, swapped baccy and cigars and the Germans gave one of our companies a barrel of beer… One of my fellows was shot, a German officer came over immediately afterwards and apologised but said that one of the Welsh Fusiliers … had shot at them.'

Above: Victor Agar-Robartes of Lanhydrock.

Right: New Year's Day entertainment for the troops including football, boxing, tug of war and a concert. From the Croft family archive.

11TH (S) BN: THE ROYAL SCOTS.

PROGRAMME FOR NEW YEAR'S DAY 1916.

2 P.M. FOOTBALL MATCH BETWEEN REG.TAL TEAM & 9TH DIV: SUP: COLUMN.

2.45 P.M. FIRST ROUND INTER COY: TUG-O-WAR. "B V D" "A V C".

4 P.M. FINAL INTER COY: TUG 'O' WAR. WINNER V WINNER.

6 P.M. GRAND ENTERTAINMENT AT THE (GERMAN EMPIRE)

PROPRIETOR	HERR WILHELM KAISER	TEL: No. 2. L.
MANAGER	HERR WILHELM KAISER JR	TEL: No. 2. L. 2.

TELEGRAMS "GOTTELPUS"

FAREWELL VISIT OF "ULTIMATUM WILLIE."

THE GREATEST COMEDIAN THE WORLD HAS EVER KNOWN, IN ALL HIS LATEST SUCCESSES INCLUDING:— "MY HOPES ARGONNE" "MY AISNE KIND DEARIE O." "OH LOR-RAINE AGAIN". "HAS ANYBODY HERE SEEN CALAIS". "ALSACE WHERE ART THOU". "DON'T BE HUN-HAPPY" "GOTT MITT HUNS"

THE UNDERMENTIONED BOXING CHAMPIONS WILL TAKE PART IN A TOURNAMENT TO SEE WHO WILL MEET JESS WILLIARD FOR THE WORLD'S CHAMPIONSHIP?

9 ST 6 LB

HENDERSON W.	B. COY.	WINNER	
ROGAN. M.	C COY.	V	
O'MALLEY J.	B. COY.	WINNER	
LOWTHER J.	D. COY.		

10 ST

CLARKE F.	A. COY.	WINNER	
CASSIDY T.	A. COY.	V MULLEY.	
MULLEY. A.	B. COY.	BYE	

HEAVIES.

STENHOUSE	D. COY.
O'NEIL	A. COY.

FINAL OF 9 ST 6 LB COMPETITION.

MCGUIRE	A. COY.
GREER	D. COY.

A CHOICE SELECTION OF WEARY WARBLERS WILL LEND HARMONY AND SOOTH THE SAVAGE BOXERS. THEY HAVE BEEN FED ON CANARY SEED AND HAVE HAD THEIR VOICES SANDPAPERED, SO THAT COTTON WOOL NEED NOT BE PLACED IN THE EARS.

GOD SAVE THE KING.

Billy was also at the front and recorded in his diary, 'Tonight we had a great banquet; a goose and fiery plum pudding. The Boche has been quiet, his only "offensive action" being that he started singing some rotten German stuff ... we had been ordered to be peaceful, though I think Boche hymns do almost call for artillery retaliation.'

William, Victor and Billy all shared similar backgrounds and attitudes. Victor and Billy had both been to Eton and on 4 June 1917, the former had attended an Old Etonian dinner at St Omer. William's relation, Henry Page Croft, had attended a similar meal in 1915 recounting in his memoir, 'St Andrew's Day demanded a banquet of Old Etonians, and some sixty of the old school in the brigade sat down to a magnificent spread in the Hotel de Ville ... after dinner the subalterns danced together whilst we old gentlemen wended our way home to billets.'

Below: Fred Hughes (back row, second right) recovering from his leg injury at Park Hall, Oswestry, Christmas 1916. Fred was brought up on the Chirk Castle estate.

Churchill

Churchill was a product not of Eton, but of Harrow. Even before the war he had been well known, partly through his journalism, in part through family connections but mostly through his energy and ambition. Having been elected as a Conservative MP in 1900, he crossed to the Liberals in 1904 and by 1910 had become Home Secretary. In 1911 he transferred to the Admiralty and he was actively involved in the war from its outset. It is therefore not surprising that his many appearances in France should have made an impact.

On Sunday 27 September 1914, Billy Congreve noted, 'This afternoon who should turn up at HQ but Winston Churchill. He wanted to "see things" so HH handed him over to my tender care with orders to take him up to the observation station above Chassemy... We went up in his car ... a 60hp Rolls-Royce. Half-way there WC asked me, "Are you quite sure there are no parties of Germans inside our lines?" ... I said I was sure there were none. However, this didn't satisfy him and I had to get his revolver out from his coat pocket, a very fierce-looking weapon which he held ready for action on his knee.' Billy was obviously impressed by Winston and recorded, 'I must say he was very nice to me.'

At that early stage of the war, Winston was still at the Admiralty, but after the Gallipoli debacle he became an 'escaped scapegoat' and chose active service on the Western Front. William Croft met him there in January 1916, and wrote about the evening in a letter to his mother,

'Winston Churchill is now commanding a battalion in our brigade. Last night he called for me in the Divisional Car and we dined with the Divisional General. There were only six of us at the table all told and "Winny" took the floor. He talked from 8 p.m. to 11:30 p.m. and simply held us enthralled... I have never been more interested in my life.'

By the end of war Churchill was back in government as Minister for Munitions and making frequent trips to France, often by plane. Guy Dawnay met him out there in September 1918 and reported to his wife, Cis, 'I had a pleasant and useful dinner with Winston last night – but what a lot of talk. I didn't get home til nearly 2am! We talked a lot of business. W. is certainly extraordinarily good at the broad point of view, not getting tied up with detail and getting a hustle on.'

146

Lucky for some

Winston was unquestionably brave, going out to patrol No Man's Land on numerous occasions, but his timing in France was fortunate since he arrived in 1915 after Loos and returned to Parliament in 1916 before the Somme. Some people were lucky, others were not so fortunate. Sir John Dashwood missed that battle, having dislocated his knee playing rugby a few weeks previously. Almost the whole of his battalion of Argyle and Sutherland Highlanders was to be wiped out in their attack. As lucky in a different way was The Hon. Peregrine Cust, later Lord Brownlow of Belton House, who arrived at the Front on the evening of 10 November 1918, just in time for the Armistice the following morning at 11 a.m. Less fortunate was Edward Kay-Shuttleworth of Gawthorpe Hall, killed in a motorbike accident while returning from leave in July 1917.

Fred Hughes had an equal share of bad luck. While based in Oswestry after recovering from a leg wound, he received a telegram to say he was to leave immediately for Egypt. Having packed his kit and made ready, he heard the draft had been cancelled. Instead he was sent back to France, where he died.

Fred had fought through some terrible battles. He wrote little about them. Perhaps the starkest reference was to his mother on 12 May 1915, a few days after the Battle of Aubers. In typically understated fashion he told her, 'We had a pretty hot shop… I seen some sights last Sunday I dont want to see again. It made me feel as if I wasent prepared to meet my God, but we all prayed, even the worst men prayed then.'

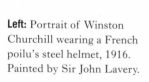

Left: Portrait of Winston Churchill wearing a French poilu's steel helmet, 1916. Painted by Sir John Lavery.

Right: *Plug Street* (Ploegsteert, Belgium), by Winston Churchill. As Commanding Officer of the 6th Royal Scots, Churchill was based at Ploegsteert between January and May 1916.

Blighty

There were few ways out. A wound often seemed the best option. Writing in May 1916, Fred said of a comrade who was in a Birmingham hospital. 'He got wounded in the hand about three weeks ago. I think he is rather lucky.' Harold Hepworth possibly felt the same, commenting to Peg, 'I am sorry to hear of E Sykes getting wounded but I hope it isnt serious, and then he may be better off if he gets to Blighty.' Officers were not immune. Writing to his father, Lord St Oswald, Rowland Winn passed on news of his brother Charles who was 'working with a fatigue party near the front line down south. He says he got hit by a piece of shell in the arm the other day, but beyond cutting his coat + just bruising him it was nothing. He says he really thought he had got something to go home on and was very disappointed when he found out how slight it was!'

Leave offered the prospect of temporary respite from danger, but it was rare – if more frequent for officers. In part this was logistical. With 2 million men on active service, even seven days' leave a year for each would have meant transporting almost 40,000 men a week. Fred saw little chance of it, writing in June 1915, 'As for leave… There are a lot in front of me, lads who have been out since November, I should like to wait my turn, and the rate the wheels are turning around now it will be a long time coming.'

Below: Corporal Harold Hepworth (centre, back row) with fellow NCOs.

Right: Photographers set up shop outside army camps and did excellent business photographing soldiers. They often turned the pictures into postcards which the soldiers sent to loved ones. The postcard of Clandon Park would have been sent by patients in the hospital there.

Even when leave finally came round life wasn't easy. Harold Hepworth, for one, found it more and more difficult on every return to that 'uncivilised country', France. He told his wife, 'it gets harder every time lovie, it was terrible parting, darling, this time but cheer up Peg and look on the bright side of it all, and when I come home lovie, we shall be as happy as anybody wont we darling. I thought I could stand nearly anything now lovie, but it nearly broke my heart leaving those that love me so dearly.'

Escape routes

Others found alternative ways to evade the horrors. Charles Paget Wade must have been one of the most unusual soldiers on the Western Front. He found escape through drawing, painting and a retreat into an interior world.

Born into a family that owned plantations in the Caribbean and of part Afro-Caribbean heritage, Charles was educated in Britain and went on to become an architect. He was not soldiery material and didn't rush to enlist. When he finally joined the army in 1916 he was considered unsuitable for a commission, despite his wealthy background and education, instead becoming a sapper in the Royal Engineers.

Once out in France, he became an orderly clerk and slept in the Orderly Room, which was a little canvas shack 16 by 6 feet. According to an account

Left: Charles Paget Wade. One of the least likely soldiers, Charles survived his time in the army by creating a private space within it.

he left he set about making the space 'quite attractive', lining it with sand-bag hessian and using spare time in the army workshops to construct neat racks, shelves and a cupboard for army papers. He 'hung up a few gay pictures … made a shelf for a few Books and even got a pleasing cover for my Bunk.'

Above: Varennes hay cart. One of hundreds of drawings produced by Charles Paget Wade while serving in France.

Although his accommodation was a refuge for him, it wasn't invulnerable. His officer, Lieutenant William Tweedy, was killed beside it on 27 May 1918.

In his spare time, Charles obviously spent as many hours as he could drawing. He chose a variety of subjects. Some were of farm buildings and a large number were of wagons and agricultural machinery, his architect's eye fascinated by the complex lines and complicated rustic technology. He also painted a series of landscapes, not blighted but as they might have been in happier days. They were an 'escape from the most terrible surroundings in the midst of all the horrors of war'. He also produced a set of garden subjects as well as 'those of imaginary places … all drawn in devastated areas where there was little but heaps of rubble and chaos'.

While in France Charles came across a copy of *Country Life* in which Snowshill Manor was advertised for auction. The picture showed an overgrown drive and unkempt lawn with the shambling figure of the caretaker between two stone pillars arched over by a leafless tree. Something must have stirred in his romantic imagination and thoughts of the house and how it might be filled with his collection became another form of retreat. After he left the army, Charles travelled to Snowshill in February 1919, found it still for sale and bought it.

152

Wives and sweethearts

Although he married late in life, Charles was a bachelor during the war so had no thoughts about wife or children to trouble his mind. Anxiety about Peg, by contrast, seems to have constantly preoccupied Harold Hepworth. In one letter he wrote, 'I expect you would have an awful day on Monday lovie, did you do any washing or not, you must not worry Peg, cheer up lovie or you will make yourself poorly and that would never do. I want to see you with nice rosey cheeks when I come home again, and we will have a nice holiday by ourselves wont we.'

Many young women wrote to men at the front, often more than one at a time, and occasionally the letter writing developed into romance. Fred Hughes's sister Maggie was evidently writing to at least a couple of Tommies and he felt things weren't quite right. He wrote to Ted in July 1916, 'I wish you would enlighten me as to who that Bob is that Mag is knocking about. Just tell her from me that she wants to stop her flirting. John Jones sending her all those pretty cards and Bill Lloyd lying sick in the hospital. I wonder if she has got any feeling for her soldier lovers, or chums, or whatever she calls them.'

For obvious reasons, women were largely absent from men's lives for extended periods. On a long train journey in 1917, William Croft recounts, 'The men were in great heart, and sang most of the way. As we passed over a bridge near St Pol they saw a woman! There was a roar of cheering. Remember, none of us had seen a woman for a very long time. They didn't grow in the devastated area.'

Things were highly different in the rest areas. Brothels were sought out by men of all ranks, though

Left: One of Charles Paget Wade's drawings of an imaginary garden, romantic and lush.

Below: Hand-drawn postcard by amateur artist George Ranstead. It features an idyllic scene and his sweetheart, expressing the daydreams of many British Tommies.

once again class distinctions played a part. Officers attended 'Red light' brothels that supplied condoms as well as champagne and other comforts. Other ranks had to make do with 'Blue light' services that were often primitive in the extreme.

It isn't possible to know what Fred had in mind when in July 1917 he explained, 'There are temptations facing us here that have tested the will of the strongest men, and most of them have failed to hold their own against the evil influence which works in every heart. I could give you illustrations but space will not allow me too.' He may have been referring to sexual transgressions, but there were plenty of other vices in the army such as drinking, gambling and swearing that might have tempted him from what he saw to be the right path. The latter three all receive mention at the end of a letter he wrote to Ted in August 1917,

'A "Tommy" is the funniest thing in the world… I have seen them in Y.M.C.A. huts etc. arguing with a Chaplain … and beating him hollow, then get up and sing a hymn with a zest that would make one think their heart and soul was in it, at the conclusion they would walk out, make their way to the canteen for a pint or two and finish up with a little gamble in which they would not use the choicest language.

'I've lived with soldiers for over four years, and that's how I sized most of them, queer isnt it, but nevertheless true.

'I haven't got anything else special to say, so I'll conclude with fondest love to all,
'From your
'Loving Brother
'Fred XXXXX'

He was killed less than five weeks later.

Left: Page from Amy Bates' autograph book. Contributions from the soldiers often reflect a simple longing for wives and girlfriends. This is signed by the soldier, along with his army identification number.

9. THE WAR IN THE AIR

Powered aviation began with the Wright brothers on 17 December 1903. In 1909 Louis Bleriot flew across the English Channel. Two years after that the first bombs were dropped from a plane by Giulio Gavotti when he threw four grenades from his Taube monoplane onto Libya. It seems no one was injured, but offensive aerial warfare had begun.

Right: Dick Bell Davies, VC, Royal Naval Air Service.

When Winston Churchill took over at the Admiralty in 1911 he was already an aviation enthusiast. Amongst his many initiatives was the founding of the Royal Naval Air Service (RNAS) in July 1914, though by then he had already flown many times himself – much to the distress of his wife. Clementine was right to be anxious. Accidents were common and at least one of Winston's instructors was killed.

RNAS pilots were quick to distinguish themselves once war erupted. One of these was Richard Bell Davies, or 'Cousin Dick' to the Beale family at Standen. Although one of the last naval cadets to be trained at sea under sail, he had taken private flying lessons in 1910 and by the outbreak of war was already an experienced airman. His first heroic exploits occurred early in 1915 when he and another officer won the Distinguished Service Order for a series of attacks on the German submarine ports at Ostend and Zeebrugge.

Their citation read that on each occasion they were subject 'to heavy and accurate fire, their machines being frequently hit. In particular, on 23rd January, they each discharged eight bombs in an attack upon submarines alongside the mole at Zeebrugge, flying down to close range. At the outset of this flight Lieutenant Davies was severely wounded by a bullet in the thigh, but nevertheless he accomplished his task, handling his machine for an hour with great skill in spite of pain and loss of blood.'

Cousin Dick, VC

In a, letter to her daughter, Helen, Margaret Beale wrote on August 29 1915, explaining that Dick had 'had the whole management of the air part of the Suvla Bay landing.' Greater heroics were to come and on December 5, Maggie Beale wrote giddily to Helen, 'You saw the exploit of the two

Above: Early military aviation: A Handley Page at Larkhill, Salisbury Plain, 1912.

airmen who blew up a station… The one who swooped down and saved the other was Dick!' This is clearly light on detail. Dick's citation for the Victoria Cross gives a fuller account and concerns an attack he and another pilot made on Ferrijik Junction, Bulgaria, on 19 November,

'Flight Sub-Lieutenant Smylie's machine was received by very heavy fire and brought down. The pilot planed down over the station, releasing all his bombs except one, which failed to drop, simultaneously at the station from a very low altitude. Thence he continued his descent into the marsh. On alighting he saw the one unexploded bomb, and set fire to his machine, knowing that the bomb would ensure its destruction. He then proceeded towards Turkish territory. At this moment

*he perceived Squadron-Commander Davies descending, and
fearing that he would come down near the burning machine
and thus risk destruction from the bomb, Flight
Sub-Lieutenant Smylie ran back and from a short distance
exploded the bomb by means of a pistol bullet.
Squadron-Commander Davies descended at a safe distance
from the burning machine, took up Sub-Lieutenant Smylie,
in spite of the near approach of a party of the enemy, and
returned to the aerodrome, a feat of airmanship that can
seldom have been equalled for skill and gallantry.'*

Dick's feat was probably the first search and rescue mission in aviation
history. While Dick took off under rifle fire with bullets 'whizzing
around', Smylie managed to wriggle his way forward past the controls and
lodged himself in the front of the cockpit. More than 6 feet tall, he was
jammed between the rudder bar and the oil tank. The flight home took
forty-five minutes. When they landed it is said to have taken two hours to
extricate him.

The Beales were ecstatic and references to him reflect their delight
about his Victoria Cross, 'Isn't it just grand about Dick? of course one
rather expected it (though uncle Cliff said he didn't) how well deserved
his honours are; we all feel very set up & have almost all of us been writing
to tell him so, the children's notes were very nice & funny; he is promoted
to Wing Commander too as you will probably have seen... Isn't it simply
splendid about Dick ... he is a capital person!... We are still crowing over
Dick... Dick's V.C. <u>was well earned</u>, and thanks to the right man getting
the reward, his bravery has got known to the whole world. Dick praises
Smylie for his fine behaviour, which fully deserved the D.S.C.' Even an
old family servant sent congratulations, saying, 'I saw in the paper how Mr
Dick as distinguished himself, you will all be proud of him.'

The announcement of Dick's Victoria Cross was made in January and
the investiture at Buckingham Palace was on 15 April 1916 when he was
presented with both VC and DSO. The occasion naturally caused much
further excitement, Mrs Beale writing to Helen from Standen, 'Yesterday
Dick went to have his decorations pinned on him by the King...I had
never seen a Victoria Cross before, it is a very simple little affair, the
D.S.O is far grander. Dick was amused that he had to go into the little
room where the King receives each one separately twice, first the King
pinned one on & then he had to run round passages & rooms (he said like
supers on the stage) & reappear; his story is the only one given in full in
today's Observer.'

Unquiet life

To Dick's frustration, he was placed in command of a seaplane squadron near Grimsby. The family, though, were relieved, feeling 'he's done his bit of active danger for some time.' His life wasn't quiet for long, however. Writing to Helen from No. 3 Wing RNAS, France, in November 1916, Dick told her,

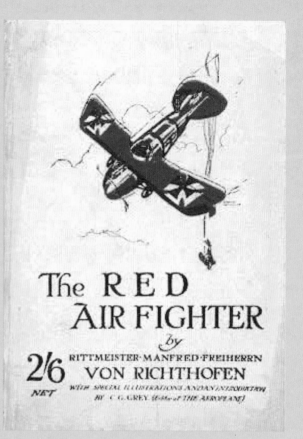

'The weather has been pretty beastly here but we got three good days last week & managed to bring off three raids. We are rather cocky about it as besides giving the Huns a good dose of bombs we had a lot of scraps with their machines in which they always broke off the scrap, and we believe that three of them were brought down. On the last raid although several got up to us & could have fought if they had wanted to they cleared off & let us drop our bombs without interference.

'We have been going for iron works and such like, but there are plenty of big towns within reach, and I think if their Zeps don't behave we could give them just as good as they can give us.'

Dick later went on to experimental work, helping to develop the mechanics by which planes were able to land on aircraft carriers. Until then, they had had to touch down on the sea, supported on floats, then be winched aboard.

Planes were a novelty and obviously attracted much attention. In a letter to his mother at the beginning of December 1914, William Croft wrote, 'The aeroplanes are the only exciting feature of the day. Two of them had a duel this morning and they bolted from each other without finishing it.'

They were as much a spectacle for Fred Hughes, who in August 1915 wrote to his brother Ted, 'We spend the time watching the

Above: Illustrated book cover of *The Red Air Fighter*, written by Manfred von Richthofen. Known as the 'Red Baron', he was the supreme aerial fighter of the First World War, with more than eighty kills. His 56th victim was James Clutterbuck of Newark Park. James had served in Gallipoli and on the Western Front before transferring to the RFC. He had only been with his squadron for three weeks when shot down. He was 23 years old.

Right: Arthur Greg, of Quarry Bank Mill, in the flying leathers essential to protect airmen from extreme cold. Bomber pilots were often in the air in an open cockpit for four to five hours at a time.

160

Germans shelling our Aeroplanes; we have seen them send over a hundred shells at one Aeroplane, and not hitting it. They cant knock them for nuts.'

When first used in France, the plane's main role was in reconnaissance and to observe artillery. It was airmen who spotted the German outflanking movement at Mons in August 1914 and later the increasing gap between the German first and second armies on the Marne in September – the latter helping the Allies to halt the enemy advance to Paris. Initially, combat between aircraft was limited to pistol fire, none of the Royal Flying Corp's thirty-seven planes that arrived in France at the war's outset being equipped with fixed armament. In part this was because the weight of machine guns slowed the plane, in part because of technical difficulties.

Once these were overcome, planes could fight one another in the air more aggressively, as well as strafe ground troops. In *Three Years with the 9th Division*, William Croft describes an incident in which he was attacked by six fighters with British colours. It seems they 'came down so low that they nearly brushed us; they then proceeded to bomb us well and good, and not only that but they made excellent practice with their machine guns. We stood it for some time: then I turned on what was left of the Brigade – it was not much – and gave them hell with everything we had got.' Although later told they couldn't have been enemy planes masquerading as British 'because, forsooth, it wasn't done', he was convinced otherwise. The machines had been close enough for him to 'see the features of the men and they must have been totally blind if they could not see 600 British soldiers all more or less concentrated'.

Nineteen days

For troops struggling with the mud and barbed wire of trench warfare, flying must have looked an enticing prospect. While many recruits applied straight to join the RFC, a large number transferred from the infantry or other branches of the army.

One of these was Arthur Greg, of Quarry Bank Mill in Cheshire.

Arthur had enlisted while at Oxford in 1914 and was severely injured in the jaw at Ypres in May 1915. Of his injury he wrote, 'I went down like a log and was next aware of a loose, horrid and disconnected feeling about the lower part of my face... At one time I thought I should not live as I was bleeding so furiously. I thought it a pity that one more so young should have to go.'

Having recovered from his wound, Arthur transferred to the RFC in September 1916 and completed a course with the RNAS at Vendôme. His flying log book is stamped '9 Dec 1916' and records that he had received a total of two hours and five minutes' time in the air in which he 'felt controls during landing' and had 'practice taking off' and 'practice in 2 landings'. In total he had less than twenty seven hours' practice.

Despite this distinctly limited experience, he applied for his aviator's certificate on 3 January 1917. He then underwent further training and graduated on 28 February. He had done well to survive his tuition, since many more airmen were killed in training accidents than by the enemy.

By early 1917, the Royal Flying Corps was losing twenty air crew every day and the average life expectancy of a newly arrived pilot was under a fortnight. Arthur was to exceed this by just eight days. He was posted to 55 Squadron on 4 April and on St George's Day took part in a bombing raid which left at 3.50 p.m.

Bombing raid

The bombing party consisted of eight DH4s, the De Havilland being the first light bomber plane to be fitted with effective armament. These were joined by five Martinsyde Elephants of 27 Squadron, with four Nieuport Scouts as escort. Two of the DH4s turned back before reaching their target, due to technical problems. The others

continued on to Etreux where they attacked an ammunition factory and then L'échelle where a second factory was bombed.

It was while returning to base that they were met by a formation of between seven or nine German planes. One of them was believed to have been piloted by Herman Goering, later Head of the Luftwaffe. In the ensuing air fight one of the enemy planes was hit but the British suffered worse. All of the pilots were wounded, but each managed to reach the safety of the British line.

Arthur Greg was less fortunate. He was killed along with his observer. Arthur's younger brother, Robert, was killed in France the following year, having been at the front for only a few days. Arthur was twenty-two when he died, Robert was nineteen.

Clearly depressed, Arthur had written to his parents about life in the trenches in 1915. His letter ended, 'This is a dirty and barbarous life. The constant close contact with death makes me think deeply. I long to be home away from these sights and sounds. Do you remember Allen of New College that I stayed with last summer? Ever since the war I have been corresponding with his sister. She writes me such interesting clever letters. It was she who sent me the Easter eggs by the bye. I think I must show you some of her letters. I stop now.'

The woman who wrote such 'clever and interesting letters' and sent the Easter eggs was Marian Allen. They later became engaged. On his death in 1915 she wrote a series of poems. The following sonnet was written on 11 May 1917:

We walked along the tow-path, you & I,
Beside the sluggish-moving, still canal,
It seemed impossible that you should die;
I think of you the same & always shall.
We thought of many things & spoke of few
And life lay all uncertainly before,
And now I walk alone & think of you
And wonder what new kingdoms you explore.
Over the railway line, across the grass,
While up above the golden wings are spread,
Flying, ever flying overhead,
Here still I see your khaki figure pass
And when I leave the meadow, almost wait
That you should open first the wooden gate.

Left: Marian Allen, Arthur Greg's fiancée. She never married after Arthur's death, but remained in close touch with his family for the rest of her life.

10. THE WAR IN FARAWAY PLACES

As a soldier, whether you lived or died in the First World War was a matter of chance. Those chances varied considerably depending on the theatre of war in which you fought. If you were posted to the Western Front, you had a 56 per cent likelihood of being killed or wounded, although even this would depend on whether you found yourself in a quiet or active sector. If you were sent to Gallipoli, the odds of becoming a casualty dropped to 23 per cent while they reduced to 16 per cent in Mesopotamia and fell to as low as 8 per cent in East Africa and Salonika.

If you were stationed in India, your life may well have continued with its nineteenth century rhythms. Writing to Colonel Messel at Nymans, Captain C.S.B. Witts told him, 'The draft have arrived at Bareilly and are shortly joining us up here at Ranikhet which is a beautiful spot some 50 miles from the frontier of Thibet, six thousand feet above sea level and within sight of the snowy peaks of the Himalayas.' His letter was written at the end of July 1916, while on another continent tens of thousands of men were dying in the Battle of the Somme.

Ironically, Indian troops were fighting on the Western Front. Somehow the War Office contrived to send Indian soldiers to fight in France and Flanders, where they often perished in the freezing winters, and dispatched British soldiers to fight in the Middle East. In part, India was the reason the British were at war in that zone, since the Suez Canal controlled shipping access from Europe to Asia and India was by far the most important imperial possession. Without the waterway, ships would have had to sail all the way round Africa, so access to it was strategically vital.

Almost as vital was oil. Among his many initiatives during his time as First Lord of the Admiralty, Winston Churchill had implemented the Navy's conversion from coal to oil. This made the ships much faster and more efficient, but it also made them dependent on imports. Oil had been used in the Middle East for thousands of years, but had only been exploited on anything like an industrial scale in the previous decades. One of the world's first oil refineries had been completed in Abadan, Iran, in 1912. The following year Winston negotiated a deal giving Britain exclusive rights to the product in return for government investment in the Anglo-Persian Oil Company, which later became BP.

Iran was technically neutral, but three major powers, the British, Russian and Ottoman Empires, all vied for interest in the region. The Turkish Ottoman Empire had for centuries sprawled across the Balkans, Caucasus and Middle East and in the Russo-Turkish war of 1877–8 had lost the provinces of Kars and Batumi. So when Germany declared war on Russia, the Turks decided to take the German side hoping to regain some of its lost territories.

Pyramids and cricket

For much of the time, the tenor of the war in the Middle East was notably different to that in Europe. In his letters home, the life of William Croft's brother, Owen, seems mostly agreeable. After a course in Cairo in January 1917, he went on a sightseeing tour with a couple of friends and wrote to his mother that 'We've had two jolly good days at Luxor seeing the tombs

Below: Indian troops on active service in Europe.

of the Kings and Queens and Nobles… It was very interesting seeing the tomb of the Pharoah and also his mother… I am awfully glad to have had the chance to see this part of Egypt – and it's seeing everything under the most perfect conditions. Hardly anyone here whereas in peacetime the place is inundated with American tourists – the usual horrors. Now you get half a dozen soldiers and a few nurses on leave.'

A few weeks later he reported, 'It has been a really pleasant place to winter in here and we've had quite a lot of cricket on matting lately. I've been getting quite a lot of wickets.' Owen was not merely a tourist. He was to see action in several battles and later transferred to the Western Front, but his life in Egypt was still in significant contrast to his brother William's in France and Flanders.

Map work

Owen's time in Cairo was shared by Geoffrey Wolryche Whitmore of Dudmaston Hall. Geoffrey was kept from the front line because his hearing was severely impaired. Instead, he ran courses on topography and mapping skills. In March 1917 he told his sister that 'the new officers' class has not started, but I have 15 officers who are qualifying for staff appointments to lecture to. They are a very mixed lot.

Right: Geoffrey Wolryche Whitmore of Dudmaston Hall shares a joke with his sister Evelyn (left), and mother, Alice.

I took them out panoramic sketching today, horses were lent to convey us to the ground. 12 out of 15 bolted at the start for their stable is ½ a mile away… When the proper course begins there will be over 100 officers and 69 N.C.Os and officers of the targetry school. 2 Majors, regulars, one of who is a Staff College man and being put under my instruction for help … I feel a pretty good fraud. I have never aspired to instruct anyone beyond our regimental officers and N.C.Os.'

Much of his life seems comfortably domestic and at the beginning of 1918 he described an evening in his hut, 'I am waiting for a cup of cocoa to boil up. I often have a cup before going to bed nowadays when the weather is cold… Roger K gave me the balance of his mince pies from home & I have one heating up on the top of the saucepan now – I hope it won't get blown off when the steam begins.'

Although he sounds content, he was frustrated when his comrades went off 'to see a scrap' saying he felt 'as if one was avoiding the job, so to speak. But I should always be a source of weakness with my infernal hearing.' His work was, of course, important. An officer or NCO who couldn't read a map would have been little use to anyone. Even so, he obviously carried a heavy sense of guilt that perhaps he hadn't properly done his bit.

Unlike many of the men based in Egypt, Geoffrey had not been part of the failed Gallipoli campaign, or the following humiliating defeat at the Siege of Kut in 1916. In both cases, the assumption had been that the Ottoman Empire was ancient, corrupt and ailing and that their troops would be easily beaten. Led by Kemal Ataturk, the founder of modern Turkey, they proved a formidable enemy.

Prisoner of war

Albert Percy Cherriman, a footman at Dunham Massey, had been wounded at Anafarta on the Gallipoli peninsula on 22 August 1915 and taken prisoner by the Turks the following day. He had been sent to a couple of military hospitals and in an account of his experiences written in 1919 he said the conditions in both 'were frightful. The food was totally inadequate and the treatment bad… I can safely say that those men that died – and they were not a few – died through sheer neglect and bad treatment.' Those that survived did so only thanks to the dedicated ministrations of Sister Mary Columb, a nun from the Franciscan Convent in Constantinople.

At the end of January 1916, Albert and a few others were moved to the central prison. Things did not improve, 'Forty four of us were crowded into a very small room large enough for about a dozen and each man was nothing but a mass of vermin. It was impossible to keep clean. Except for the bread it was impossible for us to eat the food supplied by the Turks and had it not been that the American Ambassador was able to get money – a Turkish pound each – and a little clothing into us I cannot imagine what would have happened.'

After about a fortnight in the prison, Albert and the others were moved to a prisoner of war camp. Initially, conditions were not too bad, but when a new commandant arrived they rapidly deteriorated. As a sergeant, he was evidently a spokesman for men of the lower ranks. Having been told that the prisoners of war should work laying roads, Albert refused, arguing they were not fit. Some were reprieved, but the commandant still selected 'four men including the two fit ones and Sgt. Blaker who was suffering pretty badly from rheumatism. Working hours were from sunrise to sunset and the food one loaf of bread weighing about three quarters of a pound, once a day, stewed wheat very watery in the morning and haricot beans or the like, a very little meat and plenty of water at night. I protested strongly against all this but was simply told that prisoners of war were supposed to be treated like Turkish soldiers.'

Towards the end of his account Albert remarks that 'When the Kut-il-Amesa men began to arrive at Afion-Kara-Hissar they were in a shocking state and died by the score.' These were soldiers that had been force-marched 1,200 miles across the desert from Kut. Thousands of them had died on the way. One of them had been Bert Charlott, a gardener at Waddesdon Manor.

Death in the desert

Bert's father was a general labourer on the estate and his son joined him there on leaving school, working in the garden between 1907 and 1909. When his mother died that year, however, Bert decided to join the army and was in India when the war broke out. He was then sent as part of the Anglo-Indian Expeditionary Force to Mesopotamia in what is today Iraq and Syria.

Things at first went well and Turkish troops were pushed back towards Baghdad but after a reverse at the Battle of Ctesiphon in November 1915, the British retreated to Kut. Bert was one of 13,000 men besieged in the town. Attempts were made to relieve them but after the annual flooding of the Mesopotamian plain, this became impossible. The garrison suffered heavily, losing almost half its force. Eventually, faced with starvation as food supplies ran out, Kut surrendered on 29 April 1916.

The captured men were then separated, with the officers sent to Baghdad while the lower ranks were marched across the desert to Turkey. With very little food and drink, they travelled about 12 miles a day, many stripped of their uniforms, boots and water bottles. The conditions were

Right: Lt Col. Courtenay Throckmorton, of the Royal Welch Fusiliers, painted by John St Helier Lander in 1916. Throckmorton was killed in Mesopotamia in April 1916. It is said that the stone Throckmorton coat of arms at Coughton Court fell from the gatehouse on the day of his death.

169

brutal and over half of the men dropped dead. On 30 September, 154 days after being taken prisoner, Bert died in Tarsus, over 800 miles from Kut. He was twenty-three years old. Growing up in rural Buckinghamshire, he could not have imagined a more unlikely place in which to end his life.

Right: Two British soldiers take a break while in Salonika in 1916.

Salonika

Another Waddesdon Manor gardener to serve in the region was Cecil Hambrook, whose father was under-butler. Born in 1894, Cecil was working in the garden in 1911 and enlisted as soon as war broke out. He was based in Ireland during the troubles in 1916 but later that year shipped to Salonika in present-day Macedonia. Greece at that time was a neutral state, but British troops were based in the country from where they attacked Bulgaria, allied to the Germans, Turks and Austro-Hungarians. The aim was to liberate Serbia, where the war had ignited years before.

All was relatively quiet until a fierce battle took place around Lake Dorian in Salonika early in 1917. The British began with an attack on 24 April but were beaten back with heavy losses. After regrouping, a second assault on Bulgarian positions began on 8 May, but again sustained severe casualties. Of the 43,000 men who began the action, 12,000 were killed, wounded or captured. One of those was Cecil. It is not known where he was held prisoner, but he did not return to Waddesdon Manor after the war. He married Betsey Price in London in 1921.

An engineer by trade, Harry Sandham had been working as a theatre manager when he enlisted in January 1915 with the rank of private. Rather unusually, he gave his religion as 'Theosophist'. As an experienced mechanic, Harry served in Motor Transport and went first to the Western Front in 1916. Later that year he was posted to Salonika.

Although in general the fighting was less intense in the area, malaria and other diseases were a constant problem. These may have killed relatively few men, but they debilitated huge numbers and left many with health impaired for life.

Harry Sandham finished the war as Captain, but was still in Salonika in October 1919. Eventually, it was only with direct family appeals to Winston Churchill, then in charge of demobilisation, that he was allowed home. By this point his constitution had been undermined. While staying with his sister in March 1920, he developed a fever but died before the doctor could arrive. The coroner found that cause of death was a ruptured spleen, previously swollen and stressed by numerous bouts of malaria. His name and service in Salonika lives on at Sandham Memorial Chapel.

Salonika remained something of a quiet sector until the last months of the war when a British offensive finally broke through the Bulgarians and liberated Serbia. Writing to his wife about the campaign in September 1918, Sydney Beale commented, 'One cannot help feeling glad that the Salonika Army has at last had a successful move. I think of all – they have had the hardest part – sitting still for all these years, & never mentioned.'

When he arrived in the Middle East from Gallipoli, Sydney had not been impressed by what he found. Writing to his wife in November 1916, he told her, 'We've come to the strong opinion that the Turks ought to be let keep this country so far – it's desert with apparently no value whatever, or else saltmarsh with less.' And he still felt the same more than two years later. In January 1918 he commented, 'it's very difficult to spot a geographical objective that's worthwhile. Aleppo is a long way off and Constantinople still further. Besides, we've already added about as much to Egypt as that Government can digest.'

Lawrence of Arabia

Sydney Beale was keenly aware of the region's huge empty spaces. Yet it was precisely these expanses that one of the war's most celebrated personalities was able to exploit. Like any vast empire, the Ottoman communication lines were desperately overstretched. Only a single track railway ran through the desert and this was highly vulnerable to attack by T.E. Lawrence and his band of Arab irregulars.

T.E. Lawrence had visited the area when an undergraduate in Oxford. Having taken a first class degree, he returned to Mesopotamia in 1910 to begin archaeological excavations. In 1914 he was also employed by the British intelligence service, using his archaeology as cover for research into contemporary features of military interest.

As a speaker of Arabic and with specialist knowledge of the Negev desert, Lawrence was recruited by army intelligence. It is not entirely clear what pushed him from the background work he had been engaged in towards a more active combat role. It could well have been the deaths of two of his brothers; Frank was killed by a shell in May 1915 while Will was shot down over France in October that year.

Whatever his motivation, Lawrence was brilliantly able to channel Arabic nationalist aspiration to British advantage. He helped foment Arab rebellion and

Left: T.E. Lawrence on one of his beloved motorbikes.

Right: T.E. Lawrence in pensive mood. Something of a loner, he was a brilliant scholar and writer. During the war he proved to be an equally brilliant, if unorthodox, soldier.

became particularly close to tribal leaders, the King of the Hedjaz giving him status as one of his sons. So revered was Lawrence that although the Turks offered a reward of £15,000 for his capture, he was never betrayed.

Although he was involved in some notable set-piece actions such as the taking of Aqaba and the Battle of Tafileh, his primary role was as a guerrilla leader. With his band of irregular soldiers supported by a few armoured vehicles and a scattering of field artillery, he would emerge from the desert, destroy a section of rail track and return into the wilderness. These actions were massively disruptive to Ottoman supplies and tied up tens of thousands of Turkish troops for very little military cost or loss of life.

Lawrence was almost unknown in Europe before the war ended, but an American showman heard about his adventures and gave a series of lectures on them. Almost overnight, Lawrence of Arabia became a sensation. Like many celebrities, he both craved the adulation and was repelled by it. He sought anonymity by joining the RAF at the lowest rank but was identified and forced to leave. He then became a member of the Tank Corps and while at Bovington rented Clouds Hill cottage, which became a refuge during off-duty hours. He disliked life in the army and finally managed to return to the RAF. His term of enlistment ended in 1935 and he looked forward to resuming life at the cottage. He was killed in a motorbike accident only two months after retirement, aged forty-seven.

Although fighting with the Arabs, Lawrence remained a British officer and remained in constant contact with General Allenby and Guy Dawnay. He had the highest opinion of both men, saying of Guy in his book *Seven Pillars of Wisdom* that 'he was the least professional of soldiers, a banker who read Greek history, a strategist unashamed, and a burning poet with strength over daily things.'

Like Sydney Beale and so many others, Guy had arrived in the area after the failure of Gallipoli and quickly got to work. He told his wife Cis in March 1916, 'I've had such a time! The re-organisation of Egypt, and taking over the whole of the western and southern theatres, has kept me frightfully busy – appreciations, organisation questions, economising troops and staffs, formation of camel corps etc. etc. etc.'

Harry and Fred

Guy was to finish the war on the Western Front, but not before he had helped General Allenby orchestrate the taking of Jerusalem. That was one of the few unqualified successes in a dismal year for the Allies. One of those to play a part in Allenby's campaign was Harry Hoare, heir to Stourhead and the adored only child of Sir Henry and Alda, Lady Hoare.

Having attended Harrow and Cambridge, he enlisted in the Dorset Yeomanry shortly before war was declared. His second horseman on the estate, Fred Fowler, joined up at the same time and acted throughout as his servant. In her diary, Alda recorded an evening Harry and friends had spent at Stourhead in September 1914. The men had enjoyed themselves shooting in the afternoon and then stayed to dinner, Sir Henry providing the best of his noted wine.

'The whole of the house was a blaze of light (& flowers)… All the young men were in wild-spirits – & I watched them in their khaki, all in the flower of their youth, chaffing & scurrying about the fine old rooms… They left at 10.30 pm for Sherborne.' Later, Harry told her that Sir

Randolf Baker had kept repeating, 'A <u>damned</u> good dinner, Harry! A damned good dinner.' Alda then said, 'You must all re-dine here after War,' but he answered, 'We shall <u>never</u> all sit round this table again.'

Along with the others, Harry had served in Gallipoli. As machine-gun officer during the evacuation he had stayed at his post until becoming critically ill with double pneumonia and typhoid. He returned to Stourhead to recuperate but rejoined his regiment in May 1916. In November 1917, Harry was part of General Allenby's force that had been ordered by David Lloyd George to take Jerusalem by Christmas.

To accomplish this, the Turks first had to be dislodged from El Mughar Ridge which had two prominent spurs. The Bucks Yeomanry attacked to the right up a steep-sided wadi, while the Dorset Yeomanry charged on horseback more than 2 miles to the base of the hill. They were led by Alda's old dinner guest, Sir Randolf. Once dismounted, they prepared to attack with fixed bayonets when Harry was hit in the back by shellfire.

Like many bereaved parents, the Hoares were desperate to understand exactly what had taken place. Fred Fowler was able to provide some information, writing to them in February 1918 to say that 'I should have wrote before but was so grieved at Capt Hoare's death I couldn't. He was more like a pal to me than a superior officer, everything he shared with me whether we were fighting or not… I stopped with him from the time he was hit till he was picked up by the ambulance. He said all the time he was not in much pain… We were leading the attack on a hill and galloped across an open space to get to it. When we dismounted for action the enemy poured a heavy fire into our horses which had no cover at all so Capt Hoare ordered them to retire … the rear lot of horses got into difficulty owing to some being shot and he went back to help them out of it, just as he turned to get behind them he got hit. We took the hill, it was a glorious victory.'

Sir Randolf wrote to say 'how very deeply I sympathise with you. For me too

Below: Portrait of Harry Hoare, aged 21 in 1909, by St George Hare.

it is a very great and real loss, as I think you know how fond I was of Harry, and I believe he was of me. I have hardly felt the death of anyone in the whole of the war so much as I have his.' His letter ended with the information that he had been 'wounded about a week after and had a marvellous escape', as the bullet had passed through one hip to the other without touching the backbone. Even so, he continued, 'I was left out for some hours, and Harry's servant Fowler very pluckily stayed with me, and I doubt if I should have got in without his help. I am glad to say he got a D.C.M. for it.' After the war, Fred Fowler returned to his duties at Stourhead and worked with the horses there until the 1940s.

Condolences

Another letter of condolence was from Thomas Hardy. Alda had been close friends with both his first and second wives and she had developed a strong relationship with the author and poet. He wrote movingly, 'It is no use to offer consolation. And not even time may be able to give that – I mean real consolation. Once a wound, always a scar left, it seems to me.

Below: Fred Fowler (third from left), in relaxed mode with comrades.

Right: Thomas Hardy at his home, Max Gate, in Dorset.

Though Time can & does enlarge our vision to perceive that the one who has gone has the best of it… I write the above in great haste, to answer your letter quickly. Florence has been crying over her remembrance of climbing the tower [King Alfred's Tower] with Harry.'

It is said that Hardy's poem, 'Men who march away' was inspired by Harry's early enlistment. Its tone is uncharacteristically triumphalist. This may reflect the poet's momentary surge of enthusiasm for war, caught up in the national mood, the penultimate verse ending,

Press we to the field ungrieving,
In our heart of hearts believing
Victory crowns the just.

There are, however, hints that he may have felt reservations. Both first and last verse say the 'Night is growing grey', perhaps suggesting a shaded future. There is also a bystander who observes the marchers with 'musing eye' and 'dolorous sigh'. Some have suggested this represents Hardy, detached from the excitement and doubtful of what is to follow.

Whatever the true sentiment felt by Thomas Hardy, when he published the poem in early September 1914, his attitude had changed by the time he wrote to condole with Sir Henry and Alda on Boxing Day 1917. He was bitterly critical of the Church for its failure and hypocrisy. Seven years later in 'Christmas: 1924', there was no hint of celebration,

'Peace upon earth!' was said. We sing it,
And pay a million priests to bring it.
After two thousand years of mass
We've got as far as poison-gas.

11. A WAR OF MOVEMENT, 1918

The year 1918 began quietly for Company Quartermaster Sergeant Albert Victor Unwin of the Royal Welch Fusiliers. In a diary which he kept, almost certainly unlawfully, he recorded on Tuesday 1 January, 'Went up with rations to the right of Ribecourt, got back to the Depot at 1.30 am. very tired'. Four days later he went on leave.

The last part of his eighty-hour journey from 'Havrincourt Wood' in France to Chirk, North Wales was the easiest, since he lived in a newly built house beside the railway station, about a mile from Chirk Castle. Albert's wife Eleanor was Housekeeper there, he was an estate carpenter and both were on friendly terms with the Howard de Waldens. It is

therefore not surprising that Albert should have stopped off at their London house on his journey, or that on Thursday 10 January he should have gone up to the castle to see Lord Tommy, also back from France.

His leave was uneventful. On Wednesday 16 Albert went into Oswestry but 'couldnt get any beer, I was very wild about it, glad to get home to have some'. A few days later he was in Letchworth visiting his brother and 'went to the Pictures, they were very amusing'. He left Waterloo station at 4 p.m. on Tuesday 22 and was back with his unit at 8 a.m. on Thursday. He took the rations up that evening and noted 'roads in an awful mess' although things were otherwise quiet.

The following day he 'went up with rations through Ribecourt, had a very rough time, shelling very bad, came back covered with mud at 1 am. very tired.' Little was to vary over the next few weeks. Occasionally things were 'quiet', but more often 'lively' or 'rough' when he went up with the rations. Typical entries until March read, 'had a lively 5 minutes, came through it alright, still plenty of mud … very heavy shelling, in two places, had a lively time. MG bullets very bad… Old Fritz bombing very bad, dropped a bomb very close to the camp, lovely weather freezing very hard at nights…'

It wasn't all grim, however. On Thursday 31 January he 'went to a concert given by the R.F.C, had a good time, no bombs'.

The Spring Offensive

At the end of February Albert had 'to prepare for a sudden move' but this doesn't seem to have troubled him very much and the rest of the entry reads, 'went to the Concert called the Duds at night, had a very enjoyable time, very amusing.'

Life continued to be pleasant, and although Saturday 9 was a 'busy day', the men having to stand to ready for the trenches, he 'managed to get some Bass's Beer and Whisky, had a good night'.

Things were about to change. That it might was suggested the previous day when he noted, 'Having lovely weather, still waiting for old Fritz to come.' Clearly he must have known of the imminence of a German offensive. When it came, it was devastating.

For much of the war the Germans had fought an essentially defensive campaign, letting the Allies waste their strength on the Western Front. Two things altered this situation. The first was the entry of America into the war in April 1917. The second was the collapse of the Russian Empire later that year. The Germans were aware that once US troops began arriving in large numbers the power balance would shift unalterably. On the positive side, the ending of the war with Russia meant their army in the east could be switched to the west.

Left: Postcard showing the technology of modern war, 1918.

With the domestic population beginning to starve and the army under-fed and reliant on increasingly inexperienced troops, the German High Command knew the one chance of victory was a massive push in the spring of 1918. In his memoir, William Croft remarks of the days of quiet before it broke, 'during this waiting period the silence of the Boche was most uncanny; not a shot was fired, and one could wander where one liked without fear of molestation.' Then everything erupted on Thursday 21 March. Albert's entry for that day reads, 'Old Fritz started a heavy bombardment at 5 am, had to stand to very busy, troops moved up after breakfast to counter attack.'

Right: Albert Unwin with his young son, Fred

The situation was desperate, but Guy Dawnay wrote to his wife the following day with a sense of elation. His letter began, 'Big battle, beloved! What has induced the enemy to undertake it? In view of the general situation, surely it can only be great pressure from within his own country, or in Austria – in either case a most encouraging factor for us.'

War, day by day

In the event, Guy's assessment proved correct, but there were weeks of hard fighting ahead and for much of the time it looked as though the German assault would prove decisive. As the Allies were forced to retreat, Albert's diary over the next few days graphically charts the flow of battle:

Friday 22 March
Went up with rations, old Fritz came over, had a lively time, packing up blankets & packs after we got back, no sleep. blankets gone to Greyvilles to be stored

Saturday 23 March
Had to move the Depot further back, enemy advancing, went up with rations, only one man left in the Coy, Batt badly cut up, got back very late had to move again, to the other side of Ribecourt

Sunday 24 March
Went up with rations by myself found the men this side of Bapaume, enemy still advancing, had to move Depot further back to Achiet le Petit

Monday 25 March – Lady Day
Had to move back … enemy shelling very heavy, sent reinforcements to the Batt, lovely weather

Tuesday 26 March
Had to move further back, very busy all the time, moving again to Saulty packing up rations in the middle of the night

Wednesday 27 March
Stayed the day at Saulty, enemy still advancing, sent rations up in the afternoon

Albert reported that the Royal Welch moved back yet again on Thursday 28. He noted that the 'men came out of the trenches very tired'. His diary states that 29 March was Good Friday. There must have seemed little good about it. His company was now down to two officers and fifty men. 'Had a busy day reorganizing the Coy … expecting to move at any time, no sleep.'

Warrior

By 30 March, as the Germans pressed deeper, it seemed to General Jack Seely 'quite clear that unless we re-captured the Moreuil Ridge it was all over.' Sitting astride his horse Warrior, he determined to take Moreuil Wood and records in his memoir that 'Warrior was strangely excited. In some strange way … he knew that the crisis in his life had come.' Leading his men across a stream and over a field of winter wheat, he found, 'a hundred yards beyond us was our own thin front line of infantry, lying down and returning the enemy fire.

'There were about twenty of us all told when I halted Warrior for a moment and looked round to give final orders. I turned in my saddle and told my comrades that the faster we galloped the more certain we were of success … but I could hardly finish my sentence before Warrior again took charge.

'He was determined to go forward, and with a great leap started off… There was, of course, a hail of bullets from the enemy as we crossed the intervening space and mounted the hill, and perhaps half of us were hit, but Warrior cared for nothing. His one idea was to get at the enemy. He almost buried his head in the brushwood when we reached the point of the wood at the chosen spot. We were greeted by twenty or thirty Germans, who fired a few shots before running, doubtless thinking there were thousands of us following.'

Jack and Warrior's small troop was followed into the wood by a brigade of Canadian cavalry. Fighting was severe, 'both sides, ours and the Germans', seemed to be filled with some extraordinary exultation. Neither would surrender.' At last the wood was taken. The German advance had been checked, at least for the time being.

Temporary lull

As spring turned into summer, the situation became less tense. On 20 May, which was Bank Holiday Monday, Albert recorded it was 'Hotter than ever, not feeling very well, went to Aid Post & got some pills, taking things very quiet, a lot of men ill on account of the heat.' By the following day he was 'Feeling a little better, temperature still over a 100, had some more pills, felt better in the evening, having a rest.' On Saturday 25 May he was obviously recovered and enjoyed 'Swimming sports in the afternoon, a lovely day, not too hot.'

This seeming tranquillity was disturbed on Monday 27 May when the innocuous entry, 'having lovely weather & a very quiet time' was followed by, 'received a message at 10.30 pm to be ready to move at an hours notice, enemy attacking at Reims.'

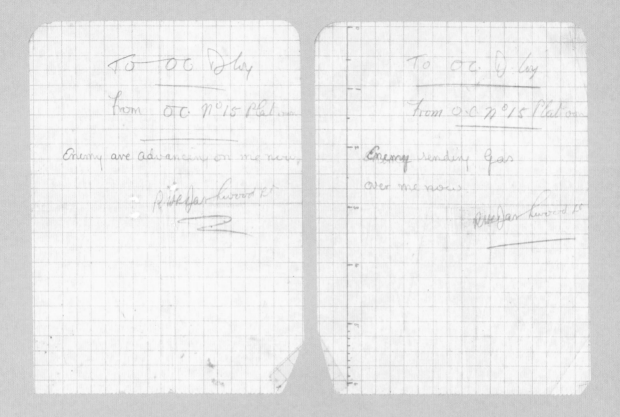

A hero all through

Monday 27 was to see the first day of the Battle of the Aisne, fought near Reims. It was also to see the death of Robert Dashwood of West Wycombe. Known as 'Robin', he had previously been injured in both arm and leg in 1916 when, as he wrote to his mother, 'One of our sergeants was throwing a bomb and it went off before it should have.' What became of the sergeant is not known.

An account of Robin's death was later supplied by Corporal Wilson who told the family,

'Captain Dashwood and I were lying out from 9 till 12 p.m., that night. Then we were warned of gas, and Capt. Dashwood consulted with the Sergeant, and we all put on our gas masks, and the barrage began. We all went into a dugout. I can assure you that Captain Dashwood, by his bright and cheery manner, kept up all our spirits. He kept passing his cigarettes round, and we had some lads killed. Then we had

Above: Two battlefield notes dispatched by Robin Dashwood. The first reads, 'To OC D Coy from OC No 15 Platoon... Enemy are advancing on me now... RHL Dashwood'. The second states, 'Enemy sending gas over me now'.

Right: Robin Dashwood in happier days.

185

sport with three candles, to see which would go out first by the concussion of the shells. When the barrage lifted a bit Captain Dashwood gave orders for us all to go over the top, which we did, and found the Germans right on us. And it was while Captain Dashwood was helping a little Lewis gunner that he was shot in the face by a rifle. We knelt down by him, for we could not leave our Captain: he was a hero all through, and a true soldier, afraid of nothing, and there was no false courage about him. He could not speak, and it was thought he would shortly die.'

After his death it is likely Robin's body was placed in a temporary grave on the battlefield. This was later destroyed by shellfire and his remains were never found.

Felix and Sir Douglas

Although he still had the occasional 'rough time' the war for Albert Unwin, at least, had become less dramatic. On Saturday 15 June he was 'sleeping under the trees' although a week later he noted, 'Expecting to move to another place, had a big draft of 328 at 6.30pm, very busy drawing rations & tents for them.'

It was shortly after this that Felix Brunner, later of Greys Court, had a chance to meet Sir Douglas Haig. On 11 April, Haig had issued his communiqué to all troops in which he said, 'Many amongst us now are tired. To those I would say that Victory will belong to the side which holds out the longest... There is no other course open to us but to fight it out. Every position must be held to the last man: there must be no retirement. With our backs to the wall and believing in the justice of our cause each one of us must fight on to the end.' By 23 June when Felix met him at Corps HQ, the worst was over.

He wrote about the encounter in a letter home, 'Haig asked me various questions about the batteries and the front and so forth, what German Divisions were in the line opposite us etc. After that he again shook me by the hand and said, "You are a very intelligent officer".' Felix added, 'Duggie looked very much like his photos. Rather short, strong jaws etc. He didn't look very blooming, I thought, which is not perhaps to be wondered at considering his responsibilities.'

Wounded

On 15 July the Germans had launched their final major assault. When the spring offensive began back in March they had broken through the Allied line on a 50- mile front, making dramatic gains. But their storm troops had pushed so far and fast it was hard to supply them, while their new forward line was not always easy to defend and subject to counter attack. The Battle of the Marne was their last attempt to snatch victory. They were beaten back.

Writing to his wife Cis on 3 August, Guy Dawnay was excited, 'My darling, The enemy seems to be evacuating the whole Marne salient – Soissons re-occupied – all most excellent news.' He was in similarly euphoric mood when he wrote again a week later, 'Beloved, Great news of the battle, really, we and the French between us seem to have taken over 20,000 prisoners so far and some hundreds of guns. A very hard blow for the Boche.'

With the end of the Battle of the Marne on 6 August, the war entered its concluding phase as the Germans began to retreat northwards, the Allies in pursuit. Albert Unwin was not to be part of this, for on Friday 9 August he records, 'I was wounded in the leg at 3.0 am by Chocques station, taken to 57th TA & then on to Aire, operated on & taken on the barge at 6.0 pm for the Base Hos.'

Where possible, barges were used for 'all the worst cases' as there was less jolting and discomfort on board. Albert was taken to the Canadian hospital at Calais, though 'old Fritz' came 'over at night & bombed very heavily, did a lot of damage'. Shipped across to England, he arrived at Norfolk War Hospital in Norwich at 3 a.m. on Wednesday 14. His final entry the following day reads, 'Still in Hos & very comfortable, going on well. lovely weather.' He was safe.

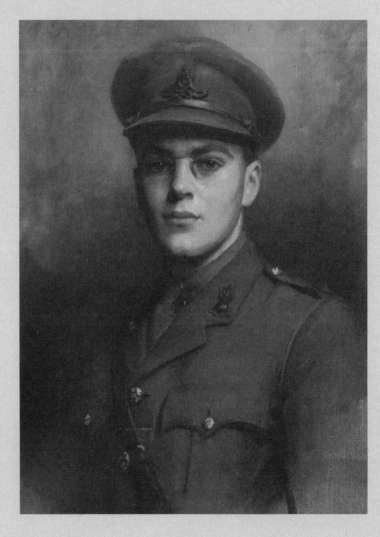

Below: Felix Brunner in 1919, by Sir Luke Fildes. In a letter to his father on Armistice Day, Felix wrote, 'During the last month's battle there can have been hardly a single day when I could honestly have said that I hadn't been more or less severely frightened by something or other.'

The last hundred days

The fact that the Germans were in retreat did not mean the war was over. More casualties are said to have been sustained in the last hundred days than at the Battle of the Somme. An early fatality was Captain Oswald Cawley, of Berrington Hall. He was killed leading a charge near Merville on 22 August. His Colonel reported to Lord and Lady Cawley, 'Your son was hit in the arm, which we got dressed by his Company stretcher-bearers, and then went on and was wounded again the second time in the jaw, and after that we could hear no news... All the Officers were casualties... I look on him as one of the best Company Commanders.'

At the time this letter was written Oswald was believed to be alive, if missing. His death was confirmed a week later. He was the third of the Cawleys' sons to die in the war.

Stagnant trench warfare had long been over. From now onwards movement was continuous, if not always rapid. There is a sense of exhilaration in the letters sent home by William Croft and Guy Dawnay. On 25 August William wrote to his mother, 'We had a most successful operation the other day when we completely surprised the Boche and took a most important ridge. Everyone seemed very pleased about it. We are out now and I am in a beautiful Chateau which positively shames me by its magnificence. I have a bed with sheets and a springy mattress. Lots of glasses and chairs. One feels one has no business here while the war is on. We hope to be out for some time but I don't expect so as we only have 2 more months in which to hammer the Boche.'

This was followed on 2 and 29 September by letters from Guy to Cis, 'Darling heart – a very good day today both east of Arras and further south. Our troops have got on a long way. The Dricourt-Queant line seems to be pressed and we have got some thousands of prisoners and other booty... Darling, these are great times and times of great promise and encouragement. The development of Foch's great battle has been wonderful.'

In between those dates, William arrived back in the Ypres sector. In his memoir, *Three Years with the 9th Division*, he wrote, 'We reached Broodseinde just after it had been taken, and from the ridge we had an uninterrupted view of all we had fought for in 1917. It seemed incredible that we had got it.'

If the war had begun with the scrambling retreat from Mons, it ended similarly as the Germans fell back. Again in his memoir, William recounts a road 'simply packed with fleeing traffic, motors, lorries, guns, and what not, all trekking northwards to put a safe distance from this new drive of ours.'

Left: Oswald Cawley of Berrington Hall pictured at Rugby School.

Like the retreat in 1914, this was hard fought. Allied troops, now including the Americans, met stiff resistance in many places, particularly river crossings. Civilians were caught up in the chaos. By mid-October William had arrived at Cuerne in Belgium where the people 'told us that thousands of Boche infantry had come through the village half an hour before our arrival; but that they had no discipline, appeared panic-stricken, and had looted everything they could lay their hands on.

'That night the Boche gave Cuerne a heavy gas-shell bombardment, though he knew perfectly well that the place was crowded with women and children. It was horrible to see them suffering from the effects of gas, for they had no masks, and they all crowded into the cellars where the gas hung about longer than anywhere else.'

William subsequently went on leave and so was in Britain when the Armistice was declared. He had fought throughout the war, miraculously escaping injury. On 23 November he was at Buckingham Palace to collect the third bar to his Distinguished Service Order, having been awarded his first DSO in 1914.

Above: Wiliam Croft with his wife, Esme, outside Buckingham Palace, 23 November 1918. William had just received a third bar to his DSO from the king.

Armistice

With its country on the point of collapse, the German army was obliged to surrender. On Sunday 10 November Arthur Hussey's diary entry read, 'Great events today. The Kaiser has abdicated, the Crown Prince has renounced his succession and there is a revolution in Germany.' This was followed by, 'Mon 11th Nov. <u>Armistice has been signed</u>. We heard it about 8 am. I received it with curious apathy, partly I suppose because we had been expecting it… A cold day, turning to rain.'

Arthur's sense of deflation was shared by others, including Frederick Hunt who had trained as a machine gunner at Belton House. Much later in life he recalled, 'On the morning of the 11th November, a bugle call summoned all orderly sergeants to Battalion headquarters to learn from the regimental sergeant major that an Armistice would be signed at 11 am. My company commander ordered an immediate parade of all ranks and told them that they could be off duty until 9.30 pm that night. Along with a few others, I had no wish to leave camp, and made myself responsible for fire duty…. It was a sombre, anti-climactic day in my life. Any joy I felt at the ending of hostilities was tempered by a deep sense of loss.'

Below: Christmas card, 1918.

Major-General Archie Montgomery of Gunby Hall described the Armistice on his section of front, remarking, 'The troops had been warned about 7 am. that hostilities were to cease at 11 am. The firing, however, which had been heavy all the morning continued until three minutes to 11 am, when it ceased for a short period and then broke out in a final crash at 11 am. Then all was silence. Combatants from both sides emerged from cover and walked about in full view. No further act of hostility took place.'

As a footnote he added, 'The final act of a German machine-gunner, always our most formidable opponent through the war, is worthy of record. At two minutes to 11, a machine gun about 200 yards from our leading troops, fired off a complete belt without a pause. A single machine gunner was then seen to stand up beside his weapon, take off his helmet, bow, and turning about walk slowly to the rear.'

After four years and one hundred and six days, the war was at an end.

12. AFTERMATH

The Britain that emerged from war in 1918 was very different to the country that had been so thrilled to enter it in 1914. There was to be no going back. Too many lives had been lost, too much money spent, too many established faiths abandoned and too many old certainties thrown into doubt. Things would never be the same again.

For many, the absence of loved ones meant an emptiness that was too great to fill. Of his two brothers that were killed, Frederick Hunt wrote in his memoir, 'both had the promise of outstanding careers- … their untimely deaths left a void and an ache which haunted my family for years.' The effect on his sister was particularly harrowing. Their brother John had been listed as 'Missing, presumed killed in action' on the Somme, but she never gave up hope he 'was somewhere alive – perhaps crippled, sightless or his memory gone. She wrote innumerable letters of inquiry about him, and constantly scanned newspaper pictures of wounded soldiers and out-of-work ex-servicemen, seeking some glimmer of her beloved brother's likeness. For those of us who knew the reality and the finality of war, it was hard to disillusion her.'

For the Dashwoods of West Wycombe there was even less hope that Robin might have survived. This was confirmed in March 1919, when Lady Dashwood received the following letter from the War Office regarding her son,

'I am directed to inform you that Lance Corporal Wilson has now been examined and states that he last saw this officer lying wounded in the head. This evidence is not conclusive and cannot therefore be officially accepted as evidence of death although in view of the lapse of time and the absence of news it is feared that no hope can he be held out that the officer is still alive.

'In these circumstances the Army Council would be prepared to consider the official acceptance of this death provided that you have no objection... The official action taken as a result of the decision would consist in the winding up of the officer's accounts and removal of his name from the Army List.'

Below: Double image of Ypres to be viewed through stereoscopic glasses.

100

Guarding sacred Ypres, where British heroism shone resplendent through the war's darkest hours

Even at this point the subject was not closed, since more than a year later she received another communication from the War Office. Dated 23 July 1920, it informed her that,

'Included in a consignment of effects belonging to deceased British Officers and men which have been returned to this Country by the German Government through diplomatic channels were certain effects (an inventory of which is enclosed) which it was stated were "the effects of an unknown Englishman who died on the 28th May 1918 at 11am. from gun shot head wound in the principal dressing station near Pontavert, and was buried in the soldiers cemetery on the road 'Pontavert-Enney'."

'As certain papers bear the name of the late Captain RHL Dashwood, West Yorkshire Regiment, it is presumed that the effects were that Officer's property. They are accordingly being forwarded to Lady Dashwood under separate registered cover.'

War damaged

For many former soldiers the war didn't come to an end with the Armistice. In 1929 there were 65,000 ex-servicemen in mental hospitals throughout Britain. That same year there were 5,205 artificial legs issued for the first time, along with 1,106 prosthetic arms and 4,574 glass eyes, as wounds failed to heal and further amputations were required. War-gas keratitis or ulceration meant that men continued to lose their sight for decades after the war.

Blighted lives often ended in unhappy ways. Poet and composer, Ivor Gurney, who wrote 'Lying awake on the ward' while on a signalling course at Seaton Delaval died in the City of London Mental Hospital suffering from 'delusional insanity (systematised)'. Alan Dawnay committed suicide in 1938 while Alexander Agar-Robartes jumped to his death from an upstairs window in Belgravia in 1930.

It is clear their outcomes may not have been solely due to the war, Ivor Gurney having had a first breakdown while at music college in 1913. Even so, his condition could not have been helped by his experiences on the Somme, while Alan may have been equally affected by what he went through at Ypres in 1914 and Alexander at Loos the following year.

Others were a little more fortunate. Harold Hepworth returned to his wife in Yorkshire but did not take over from his father as gamekeeper at Nostell Priory. Instead he kept the Spread Eagle pub in the village, though his lungs had been damaged by gas and he died at the age of fifty-seven. Albert Unwin recovered from his wound and returned to Chirk Castle. Although he had a large hole in his leg, he was not disabled and retired only when Lord Howard de Walden's lease expired in 1946.

Lord Tommy was perhaps more affected by the war than his carpenter. He had begun writing a long letter to his son while in Gallipoli in case he failed to return. He resumed it in France in 1917. Towards its end he wrote, 'Though most of my own dreams have gone to ruin, I still believe we have the makings of big men in us.' He concluded, 'You must forgive a father the childish tendency to provide good advice. Think nothing of what I have said. Your soul is your own and in due time you will account for it. God be with you.'

In November 1921 he added a postscript, full equally of affection and melancholy. He told his son, 'There is nothing so wearisome as yesterday… And only yesterday I was writing to you in a tragic vein it appears. Well, the father that so wrote to you died as he expected to die. The one that writes to you now is no more than a husk, living on a life he finds infinitely wearisome. It would have been a great deal better if I had died, John, better for both of us. But the game has to be played out. And there isn't much of value or interest to be found in the ashes of life.'

Above: Some of the Chirk Castle gardeners, *c*.1914. Many did not come back from the war.

Above: The Chirk Castle kitchen gardens covered twenty-six acres, with extensive glasshouses.

Lord Howard de Walden was one of the world's richest men and entertained royalty at Chirk. It is said, though, that he held himself slightly apart from the gatherings and appeared not to enjoy them fully. It is possible he felt a degree of guilt for the numbers of local men killed during the war. Like many others he had encouraged estate employees to enlist, as well as colliers and other workers. Where they were to be earning less in the army than in their former jobs, he promised to make up the difference so they would not be out of pocket fighting for their country.

Many of the men failed to return. Before the war the large kitchen garden at Chirk had supplied all the castle needs and employed more than thirty men. So few came back that Lord Tommy could not bear to reopen the garden and the land was given to the local council for housing.

Counting the cost

Estates across the country suffered similarly. In the North East, the Stokoe brothers, both joiners at Wallington, had been killed within weeks of one another on the Somme. At nearby Cragside, the gamekeeper, William Avery, had lost his son Reginald. His colleague, the assistant gamekeeper Andrew Richardson, had two sons die in the war. James was killed in November 1916 aged twenty. His brother William was killed three months later aged twenty-six. In Suffolk, the gardener at Ickworth, John Crack, had two sons killed, Thomas and Oliver. In Kent, James Hyder, a wagoner on one of the Ightham Mote farms, also lost two boys, Frank and Alfred.

The same story was repeated endlessly. As at Chirk; the gardens at Ightham Mote also suffered. Although on a less grand scale, they had required a Head Gardener, seven under gardeners and two part-time men from the farms to do the rough digging, and provided vegetables and herbs as well as fruits for the table including cherries, nectarines, pears, peaches, greengages and plums. There was also an herbaceous border to provide cut flowers for the house along with lawns and shrubberies to care for, an apple orchard and nut plantation.

Eventually, as men enlisted or were conscripted, care of the gardens was left to Fred Leftley, helped occasionally by his brother Charlie, and Mary Ann Baldwin who lived in Laundry Cottage. After the war the missing staff were not replaced. The vegetable and walled gardens were still well kept but the top pond began to deteriorate and it was hard work keeping the paths clear.

Estates everywhere were falling into disrepair. In part this was due to punishing taxation levels. At the start of the war income tax was 6 per cent and super tax 8 per cent. By November 1914 this had doubled to 12 per cent and 16 per cent respectively and by 1918 income tax stood at 30 per cent and super tax at over 50 per cent. By 1916–17 Viscount Clifden at Lanhydrock was paying £6,553. 12s. 10d in super tax alone while other taxes cut into his income. On top of this he owned shares in several major rail companies and lost income when railways were requisitioned by the state.

Given rising levels of tax and increased costs, economies had to be made. By 1916, spending on the estate at Lanhydrock had been reduced from £10,000 in 1913 to £7,750. Lanhydrock survived, despite the loss of Viscount Clifden's heir, Tommy Agar-Robartes in 1915. Many estates went under and it has been estimated that between 1918 and 1921 a quarter of all acreage in Britain changed hands.

Bought and sold

This is a difficult statistic to verify, but there certainly seems to have been significant buying and selling of property during the war years and immediately after. Croft Castle was sold in 1923 following the death during the war of its owner Herbert Kevill-Davies. It was bought back by the Croft family, which had previously owned it for several hundred years before selling it in the eighteenth century. Having lived at Greys Court for many generations, the Stapletons sold it after to the war to the Flemings who in turn sold it to Sir Felix Brunner two years later.

Stonehenge was sold by the Antrobus family in 1915 following the death of the heir; Beningbrough Hall was sold by Guy in 1916. Having been rented since 1902, Lindisfarne Castle was bought by Edward Hudson in 1918, but he then sold it only three years later. Virginia Woolf bought Monk's House in 1919, the same year that Charles Paget Wade bought Snowshill Manor, while more modestly William Straw bought his house in Blyth Grove, Worksop in 1920. The Churchills acquired Chartwell in 1922, while T.E. Lawrence first rented Clouds Hill in 1923 and then purchased it in 1925.

The reasons why each were bought and sold will have a separate story, but they form a pattern of unsettlement around the war years. When Sir John Dashwood returned to West Wycombe Park in 1919, he faced a bleak outlook. The estate was heavily mortgaged. And due in part to the agricultural depression at the end of the previous century but as much to the absence of skilled men lost during the war, the house, farms and village were all in a dilapidated condition.

Sir John decided to sell, but at an auction in July 1922 there was only a single of bid of £10,000. He withdrew the property from sale and when he married at the end of that year, he found his new wife loved the house. Although he remained indifferent to its charm and tried to leave many times, Helen persevered, preserving and restoring it over the following four decades.

Picking up the pieces

Snowshill Manor was in an even worse condition. Originally a late medieval building with subsequent additions, it had more recently been rented by a tenant farmer and become little more than a hovel. Charles spent several years having it restored, before moving there in 1923. He used the house as a showcase for his miscellany of artefacts, choosing to live beside it in a converted cottage.

He acquired anything that appealed to his sense of design, colour and workmanship including a collection of old bicycles, a number of ancient musical instruments, several suits of samurai armour, oriental furniture and religious carvings. Although he had begun amassing these things before 1914, it is hard not to think that in some way he was trying to save the objects from the wreckage of a world that had been swept away by the war.

Charles had something in common with William Straw of Worksop. They were from very different backgrounds, but William was equally intent on preserving the past. Having spent the previous years on its decoration, William Senior and his wife Florence finally moved into their new house with their younger son, Walter in 1923. By then it was fitted

out in the latest provincial fashion and with electricity and internal plumbing, though not yet a bath.

When William died suddenly in 1932, the house was left as he had known it. William Junior returned to live there with his mother and brother in 1938, but she died the following year. Thereafter, little was changed in it at all. William Jnr was opposed to innovation and wouldn't permit Walter a wireless, telephone or television. When his younger brother bought a car, William refused to let him park outside the house and bought a small field opposite so it could be left behind a hedge.

Like Charles, William had a strong curatorial instinct and, also like him, had begun to catalogue the various objects in his house. To this extent it is reasonable to suppose he felt his home in Blyth Grove might come to be of historical interest. Yet it would also seem that on one level at least, he was trying to create some sort of anchor, a place of security in times of deep uncertainty. The apparent stability of his Edwardian childhood had gone, his young manhood had been spent in the war and by the 1930s another war threatened. Blyth Grove represented seeming permanence amid apparent chaos.

Below: Embroidered bed hanging by Rachel Kay-Shuttleworth, Gawthorpe Hall. Rachel's two brothers were killed within months of one another in 1917. Work on the embroidery must have provided a sense of order and continuity. It had begun in 1909 and was finished as the war ended.

Reparations

The war that had been fought to end all wars looked ever more likely to provoke a second major conflict. Lord Lothian of Blickling Hall was present at Versailles when the draft treaty was presented to the German delegation. He later said, 'At the start everybody felt a little sympathy for the Hun' but that after the German Foreign Minister had finished, 'most people were almost anxious to recommence the war'.

Lord Lothian claimed that 'the permanent clauses were on the whole moderate, and Lloyd George in particular wanted to see them moderate.' It was over the 'fundamental question of reparations' that problems arose. This had been foreseen by Arthur Hussey as early as March 1917 when he wrote to Gertrude, 'The Germans are indeed laying up for themselves a terrible retribution. I suppose they will hope for peace before that comes, but the French will want a bit of their own back, and for every village they burn, more retribution or indemnity will be exacted.'

In the event, with millions of French lives lost and its soil desecrated, France was determined to exact what it could from the Germans. There were other problems. The German industrial heartland of the Rhine had been occupied by the Allies as part of the reparations. William Croft had been involved with the army of occupation and in *Three Years with the 9th Division* had written in 1919 of the war's ending,

'The High Command was getting ready to administer the absolute punch which would have caused an utter debacle. So we felt that it was a pity he didn't get his punch, the Boche. And since coming into Germany, we have found no cause to alter our opinion for he has been lately talking very big about his unbeaten heroes.'

League of Nations

Some, like Lord Stamford of Dunham Massey, placed their hope in the newly founded League of Nations. Another supporter was Lord Lothian who wrote in 1919,

'The question of whether or not we are going to have a League of Nations is hanging in the balance, and depends on whether America is going to throw herself into the proposition or is going back to the old policy of isolation… It seems to me very doubtful whether they see the necessity for this now and whether we shall not have to go through a period of international chaos … before America realises it can't stand out of responsibilities of international government.'

Others were contemptuous, Henry Page Croft writing in *My Life of Strife*, fulminated,

'Great Britain ... proceeded to go "international" and our great country, which had been saved by the valour and patriotism of our people, was deliberately encouraged to rely for its safety upon a hotch-potch collection of small states embodied in what was never a world League of Nations but a League of some nations based not on defensive force but on pious resolutions which were endorsed by ceaseless chatter at many conferences.'

Croft felt Winston Churchill's opposition to rising German militarism and demand for rearmament was the only option.

They were in turn opposed by Nancy Astor, who as part of the 'Cliveden Set' advocated a policy of appeasement. Her pro-German sympathies meant that in time she came to be known as 'The Member for Berlin', but many shared her views. Some supported Hitler because they saw him as an ally against Bolshevism, others because they shared his hatred of the Jews, but many simply because they were desperate to avoid another war. They feared it would be deadlier even than the last.

Right: Victory Pageant, Shipbourne, Kent. It's likely the picture is one of many celebratory pageants held across the country in 1919. Betty Coyler-Fergusson of Ightham Mote is fourth from left, middle row.

A new order?

By the early 1930s, the confident hopes some had had for the post-war world were looking thin. They had been expressed by Captain Geoffrey Wolryche Whitmore of Dudmaston Hall in March 1917 when he had written to his father from Egypt that,

'I often wonder if people living at home realise what a vast change of ideas has taken place in the minds of all of us who have been away so long. Those who were well off and did what they liked have quite made up their minds that the old order has gone for good, and the ones who were less well off are determined to enjoy life more if possible so the sensible thing is to face the facts to avoid disappointment afterwards.'

This sense that a new order was coming into being had been articulated by the Reverend Charles H. Mylne, MA, when he wrote in the Overton with Shipton parish magazine about the sale of Beningbrough Hall by the Dawnays.

Left: Mr Straw's House in Nottinghamshire provides a great example of domestic life in Britain in the 1920s.

'Here is the last month of the year, and we shall do well to look back and see what it has held for us. So much has happened and is happening about us, that it is not easy to see clearly. Of one thing we are all conscious – that we are making history at a great pace… It is clear that we are fashioning a new world, a new Empire, a new England, and we trust that all will eventually be better than anything we have known before. But in the great things that are happening, we are not being allowed in Shipton to escape our share of the changes which are coming. We used to say in the country that things change little. We cannot say it now. War is changing not only our home life but the social life of the community as well.'

Guy Dawnay had been obliged to sell Beningbrough Hall for a combination of reasons, including punitive death duties and the fact that his life when not on active service was based in London. He shared the Reverend Mylne's sense that the world after the war had to be a different place. Writing to Cis from France about industrial unrest in Britain in

September 1918, he gave the opinion that, 'A govt which allows conditions to get into a state in which they want to strike, while <u>at the same</u> time allowing old Hugh Bell and his like to make millions a year – is, well, not governing properly! My people who take parties of war workers and so on round, in this country, tell me that their visitors aren't revolutionary, but they mean to abolish <u>that</u> system.'

Above: The Dawnay family crest on the gate to the Walled Garden at Beningbrough Hall.

Tough times

Strikes had been a major problem throughout the war, nearly a million workers having taken part in 588 in 1917 alone. Discontent was caused by the fact that the cost of living had risen by 75 per cent during the war, and that while workers in vital industries such as munitions and mining received high wages, those in factories dependent on imported goods were affected by shipping losses. Those places could not compete and rates of pay were far lower.

Had Fred Hughes survived the war and returned to his job as a collier, he might well have come out on strike in 1921 as miners protested against a cut in pay. He may have been out again in 1926 when they precipitated a general strike. By then, miners' pay had fallen from £6 in 1919 to less than £4 per week, while mine owners had attempted to sustain profits in a declining market by imposing longer working hours as well as pay cuts. The General Strike only lasted a few days, but the miners held out for months before hunger drove most back to work.

Unemployment was widespread. After the war's end there was a scramble for jobs. In March 1919, Edward King wrote to Colonel Messel at Nymans requesting a reference. He said, 'You may remember that I spoke to you about my idea of Tea – planting in India – I am sorry to say that I cannot get the job, owing to the fact that the Firms are obliged to take back a large number of men, who left them to join the Army in 1914. I am however, in communication with regard to "Forestry in Burma". They appear to want boys of my age, and only those who have been through a Public school education.'

A similar letter was sent to Arthur Hussey at Scotney by a former comrade who complained, 'As you know it is very hard to get a good job these days in civil life, half the people one asks turn up their nose at the mention of army. Apparently the war is forgotten by the very people who owe us their existence.' The country they had fought for seemed to have turned its back on many ex-servicemen. Resentment ran deep.

As unemployment continued to worsen, resentment turned to anger. Many former soldiers were living in poor housing, without a job and often lacking the war service pensions they were due. At the first Remembrance Day ceremony at which symbolic poppies were on display in 1921, ex-servicemen held a protest. They did not wish to show disrespect of the dead but were demanding respect for those who had fought yet were now in poverty, despite everything they had sacrificed. They had not found employment or homes fit for heroes, or even the gratitude of the nation.

Remembering the dead

The first Service of Remembrance at the Cenotaph, designed by Edwin Lutyens, had been in 1919. The monument is haunting in its simplicity, with a simple wreath at either end. Its inscription reads, 'The Glorious Dead', words chosen by David Lloyd George.

Much of the ceremony's ritual had been devised by George Curzon of Kedleston Hall. As a former Viceroy of India and having overseen many magnificent imperial occasions, he was expected to select something full of pomp. Instead, what he chose was carefully understated, centred on two minutes of silence and a playing of the 'Last Post'. He also arranged the interment of the unknown soldier at Westminster Abbey where he insisted that places of distinction should be given 'not to society ladies or the wives of dignitaries, but to the selected widows and mothers of those who had fallen, especially those in the humbler ranks'.

The same understatement and equal respect for all, regardless of social rank, characterised the work of the Imperial War Graves Commission, chaired after the war by Winston Churchill. Its policy was guided by Sir Fabian Ware who from an early point of the conflict had argued that the bodies of the fallen should remain at or near the place they fell. In part, this was due to purely practical considerations, the cost and logistical complexity of repatriating the dead being considerable. As importantly, it was seen as fundamentally equitable. Since only the wealthiest could afford to have the bodies of their loved ones returned home, it was felt unfair that those of the less well-off should remain abroad. Men of all classes were fighting and dying together. It was decided they should be buried beside one another as well.

This was considered, by some at least, as an infringement of the very liberty for which the men had died. Equally unpopular was the decision to have a common tombstone marking each grave. All were identical in size and design, with the same choice of epitaph. The only concession to individual preference was a short inscription that could be added if paid for privately.

Several of the epitaphs were proposed by Rudyard Kipling who acted as literary adviser to the War Graves Commission. Earlier, in 1917, he had helped King George V revise the letter being sent from the monarch to all bereaved families. And it was he who suggested words from Ecclesiastes, 'Their Name Liveth For Evermore', which is found on the Stones of Remembrance in larger cemeteries; as well as the phrase 'A Soldier of the Great War Known Unto God' for the bodies of those soldiers buried without identification.

Kipling also proposed the inscription on the Menin Gate that reads, 'HERE ARE RECORDED NAMES OF OFFICERS AND MEN WHO FELL IN THE YPRES SALIENT BUT TO WHOM THE FORTUNE OF WAR DENIED THE KNOWN AND HONOURED BURIAL GIVEN TO THEIR COMRADES IN DEATH.' This memorial records the names of 54,986 soldiers who were killed on the Salient and had no known grave.

Above: William Croft attended the first annual reunion dinner of the 9th Division with whom he served for three years. Many ex-soldiers felt the only people who could understand what they had been through were old comrades. Reunions became an important way to share reminiscences and keep alive the memory of those that had fallen.

In foreign fields

Rudyard Kipling had particular reason to feel strongly about the men whose bodies were never found, since his son John's was missing. When the Commission was discussing the possibility of allocating each of these men an empty plot in the cemetery, he dismissed the idea, calling them 'dud graves'. In the event, economy proved as strong an argument, the cost of so much extra land being unaffordable.

The work of the Imperial War Graves Commission was meticulous. Every effort was made to establish where bodies might be buried and identify them when found. An indication of this care and sensitivity is evident in a letter sent to Lady Dashwood in November 1919.

'In spite of a thorough and methodical search made by Working Parties specially detailed for the purpose near Armifontaine and Berry-au-Bac where Captain RH Dashwood was killed, no trace of the grave can be found. It is possible that a grave once existed but owing to the heavy shelling to which this area has been subjected all trace of the grave may have been obliterated.

'It is the intention of the Commission to erect memorials to those officers and men whose graves cannot be found in the most suitable British Cemetery near the place where they are supposed to have fallen. The precise form which this memorial will take is not yet decided but you may be assured that the dead who have no resting-place will be honoured equally with the others, and that each case will be dealt with upon full consideration of its merits as regards the site and the place of the memorial.'

These memorials were designed by some of the pre-eminent architects of the age, including Sir Edwin Lutyens, Sir Herbert Baker and Sir Reginald Blomfield, while Gertrude Jekyll advised on cemetery landscaping. Lutyens had begun work at Castle Drogo for Julius Drewe before the war and resumed it afterwards. He had also spent much time at Lindisfarne Castle, redesigning the old fort into a more comfortable home. There are many who believe his conception of the memorial building at Thiepval was at least in part inspired by the Victorian lime kilns situated near the edge of the island, below the castle. Certainly their austere beauty and linked arches provide a hint of the solemn memorial structure on the Somme.

The Commission's task was daunting. By 1918 there were at least 587,000 known graves and a further 559,000 casualties who had no identified resting place. Financial constraints had at one time made it likely the headstones would have to be reduced in size, but the development of mass-production techniques meant costs could be reduced and eventually more than four thousand were being shipped to the Continent a week.

In memoriam

If the Commission represented the official face of commemoration, there were many private contributions. At Chirk Castle, Lord Howard de Walden commissioned Eric Gill, one of the great British sculptors of his generation, to carve the local war memorial. A former mining village, Chirk is not a large place. Yet there are sixty-five names listed on Gill's monument. Frederick Hughes's appears at the base of one side, covered each November by new poppy wreaths.

Other memorials took the form of land. Peace Howe was given to the National Trust in memory of the men of Keswick who had fallen. In 1923 the Fell and Rock Climbing Club of the English Lake District presented the Trust with almost 2,000 acres of fells and mountain peaks in remembrance of its members who had given their lives.

That same year, Midsummer Hill in the Malvern Hills was donated by the Reverend and Mrs H.L. Somers-Cocks in memory of their son who had been killed, while in Devon a one-acre field known as 'Mount Pleasant' was given to the trust by Mrs C.L. Hamlyn to remember the men of Clovelly who had died.

Stanley Spencer

One of the great works of commemoration was Stanley Spencer's series of paintings at the Sandham Memorial Chapel, in Hampshire. Nominally, the chapel was dedicated to Harry Sandham who had served in Salonika, but died of illness contracted on campaign shortly after the war ended. Harry was the brother of Mary Behrend, who, with her husband John, were two of Stanley's principal patrons. Yet the dedication to him was almost an afterthought. The huge work was not driven by a desire to remember the particular life of a lost sibling, but the fulfilment of Stanley's artistic vision.

The Behrends were not immensely wealthy, but they were abundantly supportive of Stanley. They waited several years while he completed other work, built a house for him and his family in Burghclere and allowed him the fullest freedom to express himself.

He was thinking on a large scale and required a building to house his creation and so the Behrends purchased a 'scrubby field' for the purpose.

Right: Detail, the *Resurrection of the Soldiers* (1929) by Stanley Spencer, at Sandham Memorial Chapel. A resurrected soldier hands his cross to Christ, as others stream past. The multitude of white crosses suggests the orderliness of military cemeteries subverted by a humanity returned to life.

The chapel was built in 1926; Stanley began work on particular canvases in 1927 and began to paint *in situ* the following year.

He had not visited Italy when he began the series, but it has the monumental, timeless quality of Renaissance frescos. His paintings, though, were not direct onto plaster but on canvas lined with asbestos on a wooden framework glued to the wall. Several of the smaller panels, which he called 'predellas', were painted in his studio. Otherwise, the entire east wall and much else was painted in the chapel, especially wide bolts of cloth having been ordered from Belgium to eliminate the need for seams.

Every panel tells an individual story linked to a larger narrative. They reflect Stanley's personal experience of the war, first as an orderly at a war hospital in Bristol, then with Field Ambulances in Macedonia, before transferring to the infantry. They also reflect his idiosyncratic spirituality. He saw the sacred in everyday life and manifestations of the divine in unregarded places. His work is imbued with humanity. He didn't paint grand generals or set-piece battle scenes. He painted the ordinary soldier preparing for kit inspection, sorting the laundry, filling water bottles or cooking breakfast.

Above all, the work affirms his belief in redemption. Entering through a door on the west side of the chapel, the visitor is instantly overwhelmed by his vast 'Resurrection of the Soldiers' in which the living mingle with the dead, soldiers rise from the grave, killed animals return to life and almost unnoticed a man hands a cross to Christ. The painting took a year to complete. It is visually complex, beautifully evoked and steeped in compassion. It is one of the great works of British art.

A cathedral of trees

Stanley finished his masterpiece in 1932, the year E.K. Blyth began another highly personal work, 'The Whipsnade Tree Cathedral'. It was inspired by the death of two close friends killed during the war and another who died in a car accident shortly afterwards. He was very clear that he didn't wish the cathedral to be a memorial, something that merely looked back to the past, however great the loss. He wanted it to be a place that was alive and vibrant, and as a committed Christian he wanted it to have a religious dimension.

Left: The Nave, lime trees, Whipsnade Tree Cathedral, Bedfordshire.

The concept came to E.K. very suddenly as he and his wife returned from holiday on the Isle of Man and viewed the Anglican Cathedral, then being built in Liverpool. As he later wrote, they had admired 'the beauty of its design and the colouring and craftsmanship of its pink sandstone' and then continued on their journey. Passing through the Cotswolds, they saw 'the evening sun light up a coppice of trees on the side of a hill.' It then occurred to him that 'here was something more beautiful still and the idea formed of building a cathedral with trees.' By the time he reached home, he had the whole plan formed in his mind. He would build not with bricks and mortar but with living wood.

From the outset E.K. hadn't merely wanted to work on a remembrance project, but 'as the only one left of a wartime friendship I wanted to do something with which my friends might be associated not just as a memorial but as an exciting and worthwhile undertaking they might have enjoyed carrying out themselves had they been able.' It became almost a life's work.

As originally envisaged, it was to follow the plan of a medieval cathedral with a large south porch of seven oaks, nave and transepts of Lombardy poplar and a lady chapel of Atlantic cedar. Over time, the conception has evolved, partly of necessity. The elms E.K. planted, hoping to 'create the effect of Corinthian Columns when they get older' were all infected by Dutch elm disease and had to be felled. Other trees, such as the poplars, failed to thrive on the soil and were replaced by limes and horse chestnut.

Since the cathedral is alive, it is also subject to change and decay. When E.K. returned from service in the Second World War, he found it had become overgrown with thorns. Full clearance took many years. 'Wild areas' are cut back twice a year to control the growth of blackberry, blackthorn and other plants which would otherwise invade, resulting in the reappearance of many wild flower species. Today the cathedral is home to more than thirty species of trees, shrubs and climbers, eighty flowering plants, sixteen grasses and two ferns. The Cathedral is now over 80 years old, many of the original trees have reached maturity and are declining. But there is continued regeneration which gives continuity to the original concept and meets EK's wish for reconciliation and hope for the future.

Two woods

Not far from Whipsnade Tree Cathedral is Sharpenhoe Clappers. This is an Iron Age hill fort now covered by an ancient wood. It was donated to the National Trust, along with Sutton House, Highcombe Edge and Dunstable Downs. There is a metal plaque at each, informing the visitor that the place was given by 'W A ROBERTSON IN MEMORY OF HIS

Above: Delville Wood, Somme battlefield, 1916.

BROTHERS NORMAN CAIRNS ROBERTSON CAPTN 2ND BATT. HAMPSHIRE REGT. WHO DIED 20TH JUNE 1917 AT HANOVER GERMANY AND OF LAURANCE GRANT ROBERTSON 2ND LIEUT. 2ND BATTALION KING'S OWN SCOTTISH BORDERERS WHO WAS KILLED IN ACTION IN FRANCE DURING THE BATTLE OF THE SOMME IN OR NEAR DELVILLE WOOD 30TH JULY 1916.'

The tranquillity of the wood at Sharpenhoe Clappers is in extreme contrast to the horrors at Delville with its clattering of machine guns, concussion of bombs and screams of the dying. Eighty per cent of the South African Brigade who entered the wood became casualties, probably the highest rate of attrition at any point of the war. In *The 5th Division in the Great War*, Arthur Hussey wrote,

'Delville Wood, or, as it was known, "Devil's Wood" was at first a thick wood with almost impenetrable undergrowth, some 160 acres in extent. The battle had raged to and fro in it for a fortnight, and now it consisted of a confused mass of broken trees, barbed-wire, and hastily dug trenches, among which were littered many of our own and the enemy dead. In the dark it was a veritable nightmare, the glare of bursting shells only serving to show more clearly its gaunt devastation.'

The inscription at Sharpenhoe Clappers is attached to a concrete plinth, surrounded by beech trees. Nearby is the Icknield Way. The Icknield Way runs to East Anglia and possibly derives its name from the Iceni tribe who inhabited that part of the country and were led by Boudicca when she destroyed Camulodunum. The track is one of the oldest in Britain and may pre-date the Roman occupation.

This is a place of deep history. The plain which the hill fort overlooks was created by a vast glacier in the last ice age. Traders and drovers would have walked here long before William invaded with his Normans, the monasteries were dissolved or the Civil War fought.

The First World War is already slipping from direct experience. There is no one now alive who took part in the conflict. Those that were children when it began are now centenarians. In time, the Somme and Passchendaele will simply be names added to a list including Crecy, Agincourt and Waterloo; battles fought over the same contested ground of northern France and Belgium.

One day, perhaps, walkers may pause to read the plaque in the centre of the wood and ponder the lives of Norman and Laurance Robertson; who they were and why they died the deaths they did. Wonder too, what might have taken place at Delville Wood, then continue on their way.

Left: Beech trees, Sharpenhoe Clappers.

BIBLIOGRAPHY

Adeney, Martin: *Nuffield: A Biography* (Robert Hale, 1993)

Adie, Kate: *Fighting on the Home Front* (Hodder and Stoughton, 2013)

Armstrong, Lieut. The Hon. W. Watson Armstrong: *My First Week In Flanders* (Smith Elder & Co., 1916)

Bell, Quentin: *Virginia Woolf. Volume Two: Mrs Woolf: 1912–1941* (Triad/Paladin Books, 1976)

Brown, Timothy C: *Flying with the Larks, The Early Aviation Pioneers of Larkhill* (History Press/National Trust, 2013)

Butcher, P.E.: *Skill and Devotion* (Electrical Press, 1971)

Butler, J.R.M: *Lord Lothian, Philip Kerr 1882–1940* (St.Martin's Press, 1960)

Clark, Alan: *Aces High* (Collins, 1974)

Clarke, Gill: *The Women's Land Army: A Portrait* (Sansom, 2008)

Congreve, Billy. Ed Terry Norman: *Armageddon Road: A VC's Diary* (William Kimber and Co.,1982)

Crane, David: *Empires of the Dead: How one man's vision led to the creation of WWI's War Graves* (Collins, 2013)

Croft, Henry Page: *My Life of Strife* (Hutchinson, 1948)

Croft, Henry Page: *Twenty Two Months Under Fire* (John Murray, 1917)

Croft, William Denman: *Three Years With The 9th Division* (John Murray, 1919)

de Courcy, Anne: *Circe: The Life of Edith, Marchioness of Londonderry* (Sinclair Stevenson, 1992)

England, Mike: *A Victorian Family at Lanhydrock "Gone the Happy Dream"* (Bodmin Books, 1999)

Gilmour, David: *Curzon* (John Murray, 1994)

Heazell, Paddy: *Most Secret: The Hidden History of Orford Ness* (The History Press/National Trust 2010)

Holroyd, Michael: *Bernard Shaw: The Pursuit of Power 1898–1918* (Chatto and Windus, 1989)

Howard de Walden, Margherita: *Pages From My Life* (Sidgwick and Jackson, 1965)

Howarth, Stephen: *A Century in Oil: The 'Shell' Transport and Trading Company 1897-1997* (Weidenfeld and Nicolson,1997)

Hussey, Brigadier General Arthur and Major D.S. Inman: *The 5th Division in the Great War* (Nisbet and Co. Ltd, 1921)

Jessup, Michael: *Charles Paget Wade: Days Far Away, Memories of Charles Paget Wade 1883–1956*, compiled and edited by Michael Jessup (National Trust, 1996)

Kipling, Rudyard: *Collected Poems, introduced by RT Jones* (Wordsworth Poetry Library, 1994)

Lawrence, T.E.: *Seven Pillars of Wisdom* (Jonathan Cape, 1935)

Lycett, Andrew: *Rudyard Kipling* (Weidenfeld and Nicolson, 1999)

Macdonald, Lyn: *1915: The Death of Innocence* (Headline, 1993)

Macdonald, Lyn: *Somme* (Michael Joseph, 1983)

Montgomery, Major General Sir Archibald: *The Story of the Fourth Army in the Battles of the Hundred Days August 8 – November 11* (Hodder and Stoughton, 1919)

Pennyman, J.B.W: *Diary of Lieut JBW Pennyman, Aug 4th – October 1st, 1914* (Jordison and Co., 1915)

Russell, Douglas S: *Winston Churchill: Soldier: The Military Life of a Gentleman at War* (Brassey's, 2005)

Sackville-West, Robert: *Inheritance: The Story of Knole and the Sackvilles* (Bloomsbury, 2010)

Sassoon, Siegfried: *Siegfried's Journey: 1916–1920* (Faber & Faber, 1946)

Scott, Brough: *Galloper Jack: The Remarkable Story of the Man who Rode a Real War Horse* (Macmillan, 2003)

Seely, General Jack: *Warrior: The Amazing Story of a Real War Horse*, introduced by Brough

Scott (Racing Post, 2011). First published as *My Horse Warrior* in 1934

Semple, Clive: *Diary of a Night Bomber in World War I* (The History Press, 2008)

Soames, Mary (editor): *Speaking for Themselves: The Personal Letters of Winston and Clementine Churchill* (Doubleday, 1998)

Sykes, Christopher: *Nancy: The Life of Lady Astor* (Panther Books, 1979)

Talbot, Matilda: *My Life and Lacock Abbey* (George Allen and Unwin Ltd, 1956)

Taylor, Judy: *Beatrix Potter's Letters* (Warne, 1989)

Trevelyan, Laura: *A Very British Family, The Trevelyans and their World* (I.B. Tauris, 2006)

Woolf, Leon: *In Flanders Fields: The 1917 Campaign* (Longmans, Green and Co, 1959)

Winter, Dennis: *Death's Men: Soldiers of the Great War* (Penguin 1978)

Wynn, Humphrey: *Darkness Shall Cover Me: Night bombing over the Western Front* (Airlife Publishing, 1989)

PICTURE CREDITS

National Trust: pp.7, 12 (top), 43, 44, 48, 55, 56 (top left and right), 69, 70, 87, 92, 101, 103, 115, 126, 142, 166, 173, 188, 195, 196; National Trust/John Bethell: p.18; National Trust/James Duffy: pp.139, 140, 154; National Trust/James Duffy/The Amy Bates/Reiss Family Loan Collection: pp.37, 38, 40, 136, 149; National Trust/James Duffy/Courtesy of Willemien Downes: p.39; National Trust/Tony Fordham: p.60–61, 127, 202–203; National Trust/George Hepworth: p.56 (bottom right), 148; National Trust/Historic Properties Photographic Archive: p.199; National Trust/Amy Howe/by kind permission of the Estate of Stephanie Duke (née Hyde Parker): p11; National Trust/Mike Kennedy: p.71, 74, 178, 191; National Trust/courtesy of Nuffield Place pp.30 and 31 (top and bottom); National Trust/Rod Stowell ARPS and Clive James: pp.20 and 21 (left and right), 109, 110, 125, 130, 135, 192–193, 215; National Trust/Peter Sutcliffe: pp.79, 80; National Trust/Claire Reeves and team: pp.150, 151, 152; National Trust/Teesside Archive: pp.72 and 73; National Trust/Robert Thrift: p.46; National Trust/Quarry Bank Mill Archive: p161, 162.

National Trust Images: pp.47, 64, 104, 123 (left), 183; NTI/John Bethell/Gawthorpe Textiles Collection: p.200; NTI/Courtesy of the Brunner Family: p.187; NTI/Geoffrey Frosh: p.204; NTI/John Hammond: pp.93, 123 (right), 175, 160, 169; NTI/Robert Morris: p.216; NTI/David Sellman: p.212; NTI/Ian Shaw: p.205, 206; NTI/Andreas von Einsiedel: p.97.

©Beale Family Private Archive: pp.14, 51, 52, 157.
Courtesy of Belton House: pp.32 and 33.
©Private Collection/The Bridgeman Art Library: p.95.
Courtesy of Phyllis and Karen Burtt: p.176.
©The Churchill Collection/National Trust /Derrick E. Witty: p.146.
Courtesy of Croft family archive: pp.107, 121, 132, 143, 158, 190, 208.
Courtesy of Sir Edward Dashwood, Bt: pp.184, 185.

©James Dawnay/Broadsword Publishing: p.82.
Courtesy of the Drewe family: p.34.
Courtesy of Gillian Edom: p.157.
©Fleet Air Arm Museum: pp.25, 28.
Courtesy of Margaret Kynaston Fowler: p.50.
Courtesy of Jimmy Fuller: p27.
©Getty Images: pp.102, 118, 131, 165, 170.
Courtesy of Gibside, source unknown: p.59
©Howard de Walden Estates Ltd: p.42
©Hulton Archive/Getty Images: pp.17, 19.
© Illustrated London News/ Mary Evans: p117.
©Imperial War Museums: pp.22, 36, 58, 62, 88, 112–113, 114.
©King's College London Archives/National Trust Images: p.172.
©Kipling Papers, Wimpole Archive, University of Sussex: pp.94 (top and bottom), 98.
Courtesy of Colin Mackay: p.144.
©The University of Manchester: p.2.
©Mary Evans Picture Library: pp.12 (bottom), 15, 67, 85, 177.
©Mary Evans/ Grenville Postcards Collection: p.153.
Courtesy of Merton Library Services: pp.49, 54.
Reproduced with permission of Anthea Morton-Saner on behalf of Churchill Heritage Ltd/© Churchill Heritage Ltd/National Trust Images: pp.90, 147.
©The National Army Museum/Mary Evans Picture Library: pp.8, 9.
Courtesy of the Parr Family: p.83.
©Royal Air Force Museum Enterprises Ltd: p.26.
With kind permission of The Royal Green Jackets (Rifles) Museum, Winchester: p105.
©The Estate of Stanley Spencer/ The Bridgeman Art Library/ National Trust Images: p211.
Courtesy of the Earl of Strathmore and Kinghorne: p.100.
©Topham Picturepoint/TopFoto: p.76.
Courtesy of the Unwin family: p.180.

ACKNOWLEDGEMENTS

The National Trust archive provided much invaluable material for this book. A significant amount came from private family collections and I am deeply grateful for permission to quote from many unpublished letters, diaries and memoirs, as well as published sources. I am indebted to the following for their kind permission to quote from family archives: Colin Mackay for the unpublished letters of Frederick Hughes; Lord Cawley for use of Cawley family letters; Cheshire Archives and Local Studies Service for Greg family material; Lord Croft for extracts from his grandfather's two books, *Twenty-Two Months Under Fire* and *My Life of Strife*; Sir Edward Dashwood for correspondence relating to RHL Dashwood; Francis Armstrong for extracts from William Watson Armstrong's *My First Week in Flanders*; Gillian Edom for the unpublished letters of Sydney Beale; the Howard de Walden family for letters written by Thomas and Margherita Howard de Walden; Hugo and Barnabas Brunner for the unpublished letters of Sir Felix Brunner; John Unwin and Aileen Wilkie for the unpublished war diary of Albert Unwin; Richard Croft and Peter Christopher for the unpublished letters of Sir Herbert Archer Croft, William and Owen Croft and Jan Greathed and for permission to quote from *Three Years With The 9th Division*; Rupert Dawnay for Dawnay family material; Ruth Johnstone for Drewe family material; Lord Sackville for extract from Inheritance; Lord St Oswald and West Yorkshire Archive Services for Winn family letters; Turnbull family for extract of recorded interview with Lady Jane Turnbull (nee Grey) 1986; Victoria Messel, for the unpublished correspondence of Leonard Messel; Will Blyth for EK Blyth's account of the Whipsnade Tree Cathedral's creation, taken from *Notes of Conducted Tour of the Tree Cathedral, Whipsnade;* Imperial War Museum for letters of Guy and Alan Dawnay; National Archive for letter of Albert Percy Cherriman.

Further thanks to Hilary Spragg for bringing the letters of Frederick Hughes to my attention; Paul Holden for his biography of Tommy Agar-Robartes, *A Very English Gentleman* published in the Journal of Liberal History, 2010; the Lanhydrock Journal, Vol 12 (available online); the Surrey History Centre for Margaret E Van Straubenzee's *Memoirs of a VAD at Clandon Park Hospital in World War I.*

This book would not have been possible without the enormous contribution from National Trust staff who were invariably patient, professional and full of information. I would also particularly like to thank the following National Trust volunteers who willingly shared their expertise and enthusiasm in equal measure. These were: Barbara Mollison, Christina Cairns, David Butler, Diane McDiarmid, June Davey, Mertsi Fisher, Pat Straughan, Peter Mortimer, Rob Bonser-Wilton, Roger Green, Sally Pearson, Sheila Doyle, Tim Brown, Tony Lomer-Cross. Great thanks also to National Trust interns Tom Bromwell and Dominic Wilson; Pamela Ward and Will Blyth of the Whipsnade Tree Cathedral Trust; Sarah Sampson at West Wycombe and John Walker of the Rudyard Kipling Society. Finally, a big thank you to my family for their unfailing support and encouragement, especially Sarah.

INDEX OF NATIONAL TRUST PROPERTIES

INDEX

Page numbers in *italic* refer to illustrations